OPPOSING
VIEWPOINTS®
SERIES

The U.S.
Latino Community

Other Books of Related Interest:

Opposing Viewpoints Series

Illegal Immigration

At Issue Series

Should the United States Be Multilingual?

Current Controversies Series

Immigration

"Congress shall make
no law . . . abridging
the freedom of speech,
or of the press."

First Amendment to the US Constitution

The basic foundation of our democracy is the First Amendment guarantee of freedom of expression. The Opposing Viewpoints Series is dedicated to the concept of this basic freedom
and the idea that it is more important to practice it than to
enshrine it.

OPPOSING
VIEWPOINTS®
SERIES

The U.S.
Latino Community

Margaret Haerens, Book Editor

GREENHAVEN PRESS
A part of Gale, Cengage Learning

GALE
CENGAGE Learning™

Detroit • New York • San Francisco • New Haven, Conn • Waterville, Maine • London

Christine Nasso, *Publisher*
Elizabeth Des Chenes, *Managing Editor*

© 2011 Greenhaven Press, a part of Gale, Cengage Learning.

Gale and Greenhaven Press are registered trademarks used herein under license.

For more information, contact:
Greenhaven Press
27500 Drake Rd.
Farmington Hills, MI 48331-3535
Or you can visit our Internet site at gale.cengage.com

For product information and technology assistance, contact us at

Gale Customer Support, 1-800-877-4253
For permission to use material from this text or product, submit all requests online at
www.cengage.com/permissions

Further permissions questions can be emailed to permissionrequest@cengage.com

Articles in Greenhaven Press anthologies are often edited for length to meet page requirements. In addition, original titles of these works are changed to clearly present the main thesis and to explicitly indicate the author's opinion. Every effort is made to ensure that Greenhaven Press accurately reflects the original intent of the authors. Every effort has been made to trace the owners of copyrighted material.

© Mario Anzuoni/Reuters/Corbis.

LIBRARY OF CONGRESS CATALOGING-IN-PUBLICATION DATA

The U.S. Latino community / Margaret Haerens, book editor.
p. cm. -- (Opposing viewpoints)
Includes bibliographical references and index.
ISBN 978-0-7377-5227-4 (hardcover) -- ISBN 978-0-7377-5228-1 (pbk.)
1. Hispanic Americans--Social conditions--21st century. 2. Hispanic Americans--Politics and government--21st century. 3. Hispanic Americans--Public opinion. 4. United States--Ethnic relations. 5. United States--Emigration and immigration--Government policy. 6. United States--Public opinion. I. Haerens, Margaret. II. Title: United States Latino community.
E184.S75U25 2011
973'.0468--dc22
2010047514

Printed in the United States of America
1 2 3 4 5 6 7 15 14 13 12 11

Contents

Chapter 3: What Is the Political Power of the U.S. Latino Community?

Chapter 4: What Social Issues Impact the U.S. Latino Community?

Why Consider
Opposing Viewpoints?

> *"The only way in which a human being can make some approach to knowing the whole of a subject is by hearing what can be said about it by persons of every variety of opinion and studying all modes in which it can be looked at by every character of mind. No wise man ever acquired his wisdom in any mode but this."*
>
> *John Stuart Mill*

In our media-intensive culture it is not difficult to find differing opinions. Thousands of newspapers and magazines and dozens of radio and television talk shows resound with differing points of view. The difficulty lies in deciding which opinion to agree with and which "experts" seem the most credible. The more inundated we become with differing opinions and claims, the more essential it is to hone critical reading and thinking skills to evaluate these ideas. Opposing Viewpoints books address this problem directly by presenting stimulating debates that can be used to enhance and teach these skills. The varied opinions contained in each book examine many different aspects of a single issue. While examining these conveniently edited opposing views, readers can develop critical thinking skills such as the ability to compare and contrast authors' credibility, facts, argumentation styles, use of persuasive techniques, and other stylistic tools. In short, the Opposing Viewpoints Series is an ideal way to attain the higher-level thinking and reading skills so essential in a culture of diverse and contradictory opinions.

In addition to providing a tool for critical thinking, *Opposing Viewpoints* books challenge readers to question their own strongly held opinions and assumptions. Most people form their opinions on the basis of upbringing, peer pressure, and personal, cultural, or professional bias. By reading carefully balanced opposing views, readers must directly confront new ideas as well as the opinions of those with whom they disagree. This is not to simplistically argue that everyone who reads opposing views will—or should—change his or her opinion. Instead, the series enhances readers' understanding of their own views by encouraging confrontation with opposing ideas. Careful examination of others' views can lead to the readers' understanding of the logical inconsistencies in their own opinions, perspective on why they hold an opinion, and the consideration of the possibility that their opinion requires further evaluation.

Evaluating Other Opinions

To ensure that this type of examination occurs, *Opposing Viewpoints* books present all types of opinions. Prominent spokespeople on different sides of each issue as well as well-known professionals from many disciplines challenge the reader. An additional goal of the series is to provide a forum for other, less known, or even unpopular viewpoints. The opinion of an ordinary person who has had to make the decision to cut off life support from a terminally ill relative, for example, may be just as valuable and provide just as much insight as a medical ethicist's professional opinion. The editors have two additional purposes in including these less known views. One, the editors encourage readers to respect others' opinions—even when not enhanced by professional credibility. It is only by reading or listening to and objectively evaluating others' ideas that one can determine whether they are worthy of consideration. Two, the inclusion of such viewpoints encourages the important critical thinking skill of objectively evaluating an author's credentials and bias. This evaluation will illuminate an author's reasons for taking a particular stance on an issue and will aid in readers' evaluation of the author's ideas.

It is our hope that these books will give readers a deeper understanding of the issues debated and an appreciation of the complexity of even seemingly simple issues when good and honest people disagree. This awareness is particularly important in a democratic society such as ours in which people enter into public debate to determine the common good. Those with whom one disagrees should not be regarded as enemies but rather as people whose views deserve careful examination and may shed light on one's own.

Thomas Jefferson once said that "difference of opinion leads to inquiry, and inquiry to truth." Jefferson, a broadly educated man, argued that "if a nation expects to be ignorant and free . . . it expects what never was and never will be." As individuals and as a nation, it is imperative that we consider the opinions of others and examine them with skill and discernment. The *Opposing Viewpoints* Series is intended to help readers achieve this goal.

David L. Bender and Bruno Leone,
Founders

Introduction

> *"Our task then is to make our national laws actually work—to shape a system that reflects our values as a nation of laws and a nation of immigrants. And that means being honest about the problem, and getting past the false debates that divide the country rather than bring it together."*
>
> —*Barack Obama,*
> *in a July 1, 2010, speech*

On April 23, 2010, Arizona governor Jan Brewer signed Arizona SB 1070 into law. Many of the provisions in the legislation proved to be wildly controversial. One of the most divisive provisions makes it a misdemeanor for a documented immigrant to be in Arizona without being in possession of his or her registration documents, which prove authorization to be in the country. The law requires the Arizona police, state and local, to check a suspect's documents to determine his or her immigration status when they make any kind of stop, such as a traffic violation, if they suspect that the person is an illegal alien. If the person has no documents, the police can make an arrest.

Another controversial provision of the law is that it allows Arizona residents to sue the police and other agencies if they believe these authorities are not fully enforcing these immigration checks. The law also prohibits state, county, or local officials from limiting or restricting "the enforcement of federal immigration laws to less than the full extent permitted by federal law." In addition, it would be a crime for anyone to transport an illegal alien or "conceal, harbor, or shield" an alien from the proper authorities.

Arizona's stringent new immigration bill became international news. It was the first law that mandated that police and other law enforcement officials interrogate people on their immigration status—and if they fail to do so, they could be sued. Many police departments oppose this provision of the law because they want to avoid scaring off immigrants from reporting crimes and cooperating in other investigations. They also believe that police officers should act like police officers, and not immigration officers. Some commentators felt that stopping people on the street and asking for their papers was too close to being like a police state.

But the most vociferous opposition of the law came from Latinos and other groups concerned that the law was mandating racial profiling. Because it required law enforcement to determine a person's immigration status if there were reason to believe that he or she might be in the country illegally, Latino activists, politicians, religious, and community leaders argued that they were being singled out and racially profiled by law enforcement. These forces worried that the law would facilitate harassment and discrimination against Hispanics regardless of their citizenship status.

In reaction to this criticism, the Arizona legislature passed House Bill 2162 on April 23, 2010. It modified the original law that had been signed a week earlier, with the amended text stating that "prosecutors would not investigate complaints based on race, color or national origin." Moreover, it was revised to state that police may investigate immigration status only if related to a "lawful stop, detention, or arrest."

Upon signing the modification, Governor Jan Brewer blamed federal inaction on the immigration issue, stating that Arizona had to act because the US government had failed in its duty to protect the state. "I've decided to sign Senate Bill 1070 into law because, though many people disagree, I firmly believe it represents what's best for Arizona," she stated.

Border-related violence and crime due to illegal immigration are critically important issues to the people of our
state, to my administration and to me, as your Governor
and as a citizen. There is no higher priority than protecting
the citizens of Arizona. We cannot sacrifice our safety to the
murderous greed of drug cartels. We cannot stand idly by as
drop houses, kidnappings and violence compromise our
quality of life. We cannot delay while the destruction hap-
pening south of our international border creeps its way
north. We in Arizona have been more than patient waiting
for Washington to act. But decades of federal inaction and
misguided policy have created a dangerous and unacceptable
situation.

In his remarks on comprehensive immigration reform,
President Barack Obama agreed with Brewer on that point.
"The politics of who is and who is not allowed to enter this
country, and on what terms, has always been contentious. And
that remains true today. And it's made worse by a failure of
those of us in Washington to fix a broken immigration system," he acknowledged.

Yet Obama argued that stringent laws like the one passed
in Arizona were not the solution:

Into this breach, states like Arizona have decided to take
matters into their own hands. Given the levels of frustration
across the country, this is understandable. But it is also ill
conceived. And it's not just that the law Arizona passed is
divisive—although it has fanned the flames of an already
contentious debate. Laws like Arizona's put huge pressures
on local law enforcement to enforce rules that ultimately are
unenforceable.

These laws also have the potential of violating the rights of
innocent American citizens and legal residents, making them
subject to possible stops or questioning because of what
they look like or how they sound. And as other states and

localities go their own ways, we face the prospect that different rules for immigration will apply in different parts of the country—a patchwork of local immigration rules where we all know one clear national standard is needed.

The authors of the viewpoints presented in *Opposing Viewpoints: The U.S. Latino Community* debate issues like the Arizona immigration law in the following chapters: How Is the U.S. Latino Community Perceived? What Immigration Attitudes and Policies Affect the U.S. Latino Community? What Is the Political Power of the U.S. Latino Community? What Social Issues Impact the U.S. Latino Community? This volume examines the challenges and achievements of Latinos in the United States and debates political, economical, and social issues that will affect the community.

CHAPTER 1

How Is the U.S. Latino Community Perceived?

Chapter Preface

On July 12, 2008, a group of seven teenagers in the small coal town of Shenandoah, Pennsylvania, went out to a block party. After leaving around 11 P.M., the group walked toward a local park, where they came upon a twenty-five-year-old illegal immigrant, Luis Ramirez, talking with a teenage girl. The youths began goading Ramirez and the girl. According to the deposition of witnesses, they demanded that Ramirez "should get out of this neighborhood," and directed the girl to "get your Mexican boyfriend out of here." Ramirez and the girl began to walk away when one of the youths yelled an ethnic slur at him. When Ramirez turned around and asked, "What's your problem?" the conflict escalated into a fight. Ramirez was knocked unconscious, then kicked and punched while motionless in the street. The suspects fled the scene. Ramirez was taken to the hospital and underwent emergency surgery. Tragically, he died the next day.

It did not take long for authorities to catch the perpetrators. Three young men were charged as adults with homicide and ethnic intimidation in Ramirez's death; another young man was charged with aggravated assault and ethnic intimidation. Most of the boys were still in high school and played on the Shenandoah Valley High School football team.

On May 1, 2009, all four defendants were acquitted by a jury of all serious crimes in the death of Luis Ramirez. Immediately, Latino civil rights groups were up in arms over the verdict, pushing for the passage of a federal hate-crimes bill that would broaden enforcement of such crimes. They pointed to an alarming upswing in hate crimes against Hispanics nationally. According to FBI statistics, there has been an increase in the number of Hispanic victims involved in hate crimes in the past several years.

Yet some critics of sweeping hate-crimes legislation advocate caution. They contend that is almost impossible to delve into the minds of people accused of committing crimes based on race, color, religion, ethnicity, gender, sexual orientation, gender identity, or disability. How can a prosecutor determine beyond a shadow of a doubt that Ramirez was attacked solely because he was Hispanic? Such cases are difficult to prove in a court of law.

Five months after the acquittals in the Ramirez case, a federal law was passed, expanding the 1969 US federal hate-crime law to include crimes motivated by a victim's actual or perceived gender, sexual orientation, gender identity, or disability. Known as the Matthew Shepard and James Byrd Jr. Hate Crimes Act, the new law gives federal authorities greater ability to pursue hate-crime investigations and provides more funding for investigating and tracking hate crimes in the United States.

The following chapter, which examines the perception of the US Latino community, explores the debate over the severity of the problem of hate crimes committed against Latinos. Other issues debated are the contribution of Latinos to life in the United States and the characterization of Latino family values.

| "The influence of Latinos . . . is felt in every aspect of society and is part of the nation's rich cultural diversity."

Latinos Have Made a Rich Contribution to American Life

Carolee Walker

Carolee Walker is a staff writer for America.gov, a political website. In the following viewpoint, she deems the influence of Latinos to be pervasive in US society and an integral part of the nation's cultural diversity. Walker discusses this profound influence in sports, literature, and the political arena and emphasizes the growing impact Latino voters have on national elections and Latino consumers have had on the US economy.

As you read, consider the following questions:

1. According to Pilar O'Leary, as cited by Walker, who founded the first European settlement in what is now the United States?

2. What is the largest minority group in the United States, according to the US Census Bureau, as cited by the author?

Carolee Walker, "U.S. Politics, Literature, Sports Show Cultural Influence of Hispanics," America.gov, September 11, 2007. Reproduced by permission.

3. Why does O'Leary, as cited by Walker, think that US Latinos share a bond with Spain?

The influence of Latinos, especially as the United States population grows, is felt in every aspect of society and is part of the nation's rich cultural diversity.

"Latinos have a long history in the United States," said Pilar O'Leary of the Smithsonian Institution during an *Ask America* webchat September 11, 2007. "Decades before English colonists arrived on these shores, Hispanic explorers founded the first European settlement in St. Augustine, Florida."

Many Latinos come to this country to provide their children with better opportunities in education and to contribute to the economic and cultural fabric of the United States where they may enjoy freedoms and opportunities they might not have at home, according to O'Leary, who develops exhibitions, research and public programs at the Smithsonian Latino Center.

"This is true, I believe, not just for recent Latino immigrants but also for Latino families who have been here for generations," she said.

The Latino Influence

According to U.S. Census Bureau estimates, Hispanics are the largest minority group in the United States and also the fastest-growing group.

O'Leary said Latinos' influence on baseball in the United States is significant, but in addition, football (called soccer in the United States) icons from Latin America have gained celebrity status in the United States and will "help with the popularity and recognition of the sport." Furthermore, a quarter of Major League Baseball players are from Puerto Rico and Latin American countries, especially the Dominican Republic, Venezuela, Cuba, Colombia and Mexico. The Latino Center

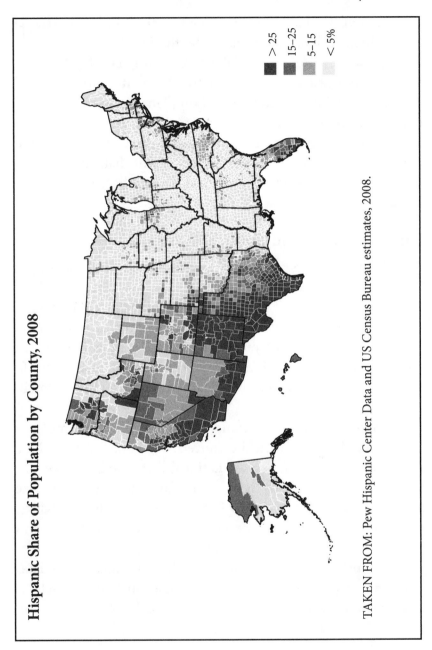

Hispanic Share of Population by County, 2008

> 25
15–25
5–15
< 5%

TAKEN FROM: Pew Hispanic Center Data and US Census Bureau estimates, 2008.

has partnered with the Smithsonian Institution Traveling Exhibition Service to develop an exhibition on baseball legend Roberto Clemente.

"Beyond Baseball" was developed by the Museo de Arte de Puerto Rico and was coordinated by the Smithsonian. The exhibition will include a downloadable bilingual (English and Spanish) podcast and an interactive Web site with a virtual exhibition, children's activities, lesson plans, biographical highlights and photographs.

Clemente, who was born in Puerto Rico, was a 12-time Major League Baseball all-star selection who helped the Pittsburgh Pirates claim the 1971 World Series, the championship of U.S. professional baseball.

Latino Literary and Political Influence

Such Latino authors as Gabriel García Márquez, Mario Vargas Llosa, Carlos Fuentes and Isabel Allende have blazed a trail for Latino authors in the United States and globally, O'Leary said. And there are many other, more contemporary Latino authors who also are gaining serious recognition—such as Dominican author Julia Álvarez, she added. Álvarez's acclaimed novel *In the Time of the Butterflies* was made into a television film in 2001.

Although the 2008 elections will not be the first time candidates will be faced with the concerns of Latino voters, there is an increasing awareness of Latinos' importance in the political landscape, O'Leary said. As the population grows in size and becomes economically stronger and more politically savvy, candidates likely will become sensitive to the needs, values and objectives of the Latino community.

"For the first time in history you have political candidates engaging in presidential debates on Spanish-language television," as well as the involvement of politicians in immigration marches, she said.

Spain and American Latinos

Many Latinos share a common heritage with Spain, O'Leary said. The Spanish colonized most of Latin America and brought with them the Spanish language—the language spoken by the majority of the Latino population—culture, religion and social mores. Latinos in the United States and living abroad still feel a strong nexus to Spain, O'Leary said. "It is Spanish heritage that ties many Latinos from different countries and backgrounds together."

In recent years, Spain itself has made an effort to connect with Latino communities in the United States and abroad through cultural and educational initiatives, according to O'Leary.

She also discussed the Latino Center's Young Ambassador's Program, an educational initiative for Hispanic secondary school seniors gifted in the arts that provides students from across the country with the opportunity to meet with scholars, artists, curators and other accomplished individuals in the field of Latino arts and culture.

| *"America is unlikely to find many creative geniuses among Hispanic immigrants—especially among illegal ones."*

The Latino Contribution to American Life Is Not Outstanding

Steve Sailer

Steve Sailer is a journalist, the founder of the Human Biodiversity Institute, and the movie critic for the American Conservative. *In the following viewpoint, he argues that although the US media frequently discusses the rich contributions of Latinos to life in the United States, they have actually made little contribution to cultural and scientific fields. To illuminate this claim, Sailer examines rankings of history's important creators to find that Latin America has few outstanding achievements in any field except for literature.*

As you read, consider the following questions:

1. How many significant figures did Charles Murray find who qualified for inclusion in his database, according to Sailer?

2. What percentage of the most famous scientists and Western artists came from Latin America, according to Murray's study, as cited by the author?

3. According to Murray's study, as reported by Sailer, how many of the world's most significant philosophers were Latin American?

The recent movie *A Day Without a Mexican* asks the interesting question: What would happen if California's twelve million Hispanics suddenly disappeared?

Some slapstick satire ensues as the state's remaining whites, blacks, and Asians try (and fail) to pick their own oranges, wash their own cars, and care for their own children.

Yet the plot makes the unintended point that Hispanics have contributed far more drudgery than creativity to California. Although the media regularly blather about the "vibrant contributions of Latin-American culture," the plain truth is that California's main creative industries—Hollywood and Silicon Valley—employ few Latinos above the technician level.

Creativity and the Hispanic World

But, then, has creativity ever been the strong suit of the Hispanic world? Can we really expect to find much scientific or artistic talent among immigrants from Latin America?

To investigate these questions, I crunched some numbers from Charles Murray's recent gift to data nerds everywhere, his book *Human Accomplishment: The Pursuit of Excellence in the Arts and Sciences, 800 B.C. to 1950.*

Murray ranked objectively history's most important creators and discoverers based on their representation in leading histories and encyclopedias.

For example, to determine the most significant Western visual artists, Murray assembled 14 leading comprehensive works by art historians such as [Ernst] Gombrich and [H.W.] Janson. For each name in each book's index, he typed into his computer basic measures of importance such as the number of pages mentioning the artist. (No surprise: Michelangelo came out on top.) It's important to note that Murray's own opinions played no role in his process.

This sounds simple, perhaps even simple-minded. But these kinds of metrics of eminence have been repeatedly validated over a century of use, beginning with [English scientist] Francis Galton.

Murray's List

The hundreds of scholars upon whom Murray relies have their personal and professional biases. But, ultimately, their need to create coherent narratives explaining who influenced whom means that their books aren't primarily based on their own tastes, but instead on those of their subjects.

For example, the best single confirmation of the greatness of [Ludwig van] Beethoven (who ties with [Wolfgang Amadeus] Mozart as the most eminent composer in Murray's tables) might be [Johannes] Brahms's explanation of why he spent decades fussing before finally unveiling his own First Symphony: "You have no idea how it feels for someone like me to hear behind him the tramp of a giant like Beethoven." Thus, no musical scholar could leave out Beethoven without also leaving out Brahms, [Robert] Schumann, [Hector] Berlioz, [Richard] Wagner, [Gustav] Mahler, and other composers influenced by Beethoven.

Murray found 4,002 "significant figures" who qualified for inclusion in his database because they were mentioned in at least half the top reference books in their field. He reserved eight of his twenty categories for Asian subjects such as Japanese Painting and Indian Philosophy. That leaves 3,404 significant figures in the twelve fields open to Westerners.

So how did Latin Americans do?

Not terribly well at all: just half of one percent of the most famous scientists and Western artists came from Latin America.

None of the 1,414 scientists who made the cut was a Latin American. That's not too surprising because the mother country, Spain, contributed only four scientists . . . and even one of those four was the medieval Muslim astronomer Al-Zarqali!

Latin American Achievement

Latin America did a little better in the sphere of high culture, accounting for 18 (or 0.9%) of the 1,990 top artists, composers, writers, and philosophers in the history of Western Civilization. (I'm including among the Latin Americans the only Brazilian in the database, composer [Heitor] Villa-Lobos.)

Spain has given the world a fair-to-middling 65 cultural creators—3.3% of all significant figures in the history of Western arts and philosophy. But Spain has been in a bit of a creative slump since its brilliant Golden Age of roughly 1550 to about 1660. There have been only 25 Spanish key creators since 1700. In contrast, the small country of the Netherlands developed 46 significant figures just during the 17th Century.

The Hispanic world's strong suit has been literature, with 13 significant Latin American writers (or 1.6% of the 835 most eminent Western writers). Top Latin American authors include [Jorge Luis] Borges and [Pablo] Neruda. Among the 33 significant Spanish writers (4.0%) are [Miguel de] Cervantes, Lope de Vega, and [Federico] Garcia Lorca.

Presumably individual genius is more likely to reach fruition in the field of literature because in the sciences or some of the other, more expensive arts, a high degree of social support for achievement is a precondition.

Art Rankings

The three great Mexican muralists of the 20th Century, [Diego] Rivera, [David Alfaro] Siqueiros, and [José Clemente] Orozco, are the only Latin Americans (0.6%) among the 479 most famous painters and sculptors.

In contrast, fifteen Spaniards (3.1%) made the list, most coming from either Spain's Golden Age (for instance, [Diego]

Velasquez, [Francisco] Zubaran, [Jusepe] de Ribera, and the Crete-born El Greco) or from the 20th Century (such as [Pablo] Picasso, [Joan] Miro, and [Salvador] Dali). The titanic [Francisco] Goya was the only significant Spanish painter to flourish between the middle of the 17th Century and the beginning of the 20th Century.

Music Rankings

Of the 522 best-known classical composers, only two (0.4%) were Latin Americans (Villa-Lobos and the Mexican Carlos Chavez y Ramirez) and thirteen (2.5%) were Spaniards, but most of them were late medieval figures. [Manuel] De Falla is probably the best-known (and perhaps only well-known) Spanish composer. (However, there have been many great Spanish performers, such as [Pablo] Casals and [Andrés] Segovia.)

Philosophy Rankings

Among the 154 significant Western philosophers, there are no Latin Americans and four Spaniards. Of these four, however, two were Muslim Moors (Averroes and Avicebron), one the famous Jewish philosopher of the Muslim world, [Moses] Maimonides, and the fourth was [George] Santayana, who emigrated to the U.S. as a child. On the other hand, two well-known Spanish philosophers arguably should have qualified: [José] Ortega y Gasset and [Miguel de] Unamuno (who showed up on the table of top writers instead).

In summary, Spain was a leading European nation up until the middle of the 17th Century, after which it fell into the third rank.

Latin America has always been a backwater of Western Civilization, except in literature.

Trends Continue

Murray didn't cover the last half of the 20th Century, but the long-term trends seem to be continuing. Latin Americans have won a grand total of only three Nobel Prizes in the sciences and Spain only one. In contrast, Denmark has won eight, and the U.S. 206.

Latin America remains more productive in literature than in other fields, with dazzling novelists such as Garcia Marquez and Vargas Llosa. Over the last half century, classical composition, art, and philosophy appear to have been in general decline across the Western world, so Latin America's lack of innovation in those fields no longer stands out as embarrassingly.

In the realm of popular culture, the last half of the 20th Century witnessed the overwhelming triumph of the U.S.A. Latin American pop music was vastly outgunned by American rock and roll. But even little English-speaking Jamaica wound up having more influence on music than did Cuba, which had been the most musically dynamic Spanish-speaking country. Perhaps [Fidel] Castro's (hopefully imminent) demise should free up Cuba's tremendous musical talent.

The more insidious Mexican ruling party bribed its artists into comfortable submission, which may account for the lack of Mexican creativity over the last 50 years. As the PRI [Mexico's controlling political party for decades] fell apart over the last decade, several exciting Mexican movie directors have emerged.

Nonetheless, the bottom line: Latin America has been the least creative outpost of the West. And that probably won't change much.

America is unlikely to find many creative geniuses among Hispanic immigrants—especially among illegal ones.

> "The most admired values of the His-
> panic community are the same values
> that sustain our nation's greatness."

Latino Values Are Conservative Family Values

Alberto Gonzales

Alberto Gonzales is the former attorney general of the United States. In the following viewpoint, he asserts that values important to the Hispanic community—hard work, sacrifice, family, entrepreneurship, and perseverance—are also central to all Americans. Gonzales reflects on the values instilled in him by his parents and notes these are the same values he saw in many Americans during his time as attorney general.

As you read, consider the following questions:

1. What does Gonzales say his father, Pablo, did for a living as a young man?

2. What three values did the author's parents instill in him?

3. What does Gonzales view as the story of America?

Alberto Gonzales, "Hispanic Values Equal American Values," CNN.com, October 7, 2007. Reproduced by permission.

Over the next few weeks, America recognizes what many in this country know from personal experience. The most admired values of the Hispanic community are the same values that sustain our nation's greatness: sacrifice, hard work, personal initiative, dedication to family, and perseverance in the face of adversity.

I saw these values every day in the life of my father, Pablo.

My father was not an educated man. But he worked every day to help his eight children find the American dream.

As a young man, he picked crops in the fields of South Texas, where he met another migrant worker—a young woman named Maria, who would become my mother.

He and two of my uncles built the house in Houston that I grew up in—my mother lives there still today.

I can remember when I was a small boy playing in the field as they laid the cinder blocks for the house's foundation. They nailed together the two-by-fours, hung the drywall, and hammered the composition shingles onto the roof. From their sweat, toil and vision arose the small two-bedroom house that became our home.

That home is my past, but it also represents our heritage, as Americans who always dream and work for a better tomorrow.

American Principles

As a young boy I would ask my mother to wake me before dawn so I could eat scrambled eggs and tortillas with my father before he left for work. As dad and I ate breakfast together, my mother would prepare a modest lunch of beans and tortillas and carefully place them in a brown paper sack. I can picture my dad walking down the street to catch a ride to the construction site and me running outside and waving goodbye.

The memories of this daily ritual burn strong in my chest as I recall this simple time, that simple food, and those deep, enduring American values of family, hard work, and sacrifice.

Those are the principles that my parents instilled in me.

And those principles are the best heritage of our community. They are the values our nation reaffirms during Hispanic Heritage Month.

I'm telling you this story not because there's something so remarkable about my life, but because of how frankly unremarkable it has been in many ways. And that's what is so wonderful about this great country.

My Experience as a Public Servant

The story of America is a story of constant renewal and reaffirmation of our founding ideas and our enduring values of faith, family, and freedom. I have drawn on the strength of my heritage and the insights of my background to try to make America a better place for everyone.

Over the past 2 1/2 years as attorney general, I have seen crimes involving dishonesty, corruption and depravity of types I never thought possible. I've seen things I didn't know man was capable of.

But I will tell you here and now that I am still hopeful. Because every time I see a glimmer of the evil man can do, I see the defenders of liberty, truth, and justice who stand ready to fight it.

I see the courage of our soldiers, sailors, Marines, and airmen and I am hopeful, and so very proud. My time in public service has had its share of difficulties, but even more moments of inspiration. My trips to Iraq have been among them. Being part of a department that plays a vital role in stopping terrorists has been a humbling experience.

I have often said that my worst day in office was better than my father's best day. My work has not been easy, but it has been unbelievably rewarding. Because I knew that every day when I got up, I was being given a new opportunity to work for the American people.

When I first went into public service, I told my wife, Rebecca, it would only be for a couple of years. It's been longer than that, but I have truly enjoyed myself. And I left public service proud to know that other Hispanics will carry on the mantle of service.

Others Must Carry On

My hopes, and those of many others with stories similar to mine, are reflected in those words of the founders of this nation more than two centuries ago: "We hold these truths to be self-evident, that all men are created equal, that they are endowed by their Creator with certain unalienable rights, that among these are life, liberty, and the pursuit of happiness."

Those words are a simple, clear expression of the American dream. I believe in that dream with all my heart. I have lived it in a way I never would have thought possible.

I am the son of a Mexican cotton picker and a construction worker who never finished grade school, and I served as the Attorney General of the United States. If anyone ever tries to tell you the American dream doesn't exist, or that you can't achieve it, I hope you'll prove them wrong.

| "Hackneyed invocation of Hispanic 'family values' is . . . laughable."

Characterizations of Latino Family Values Are Flawed

Heather Mac Donald

Heather Mac Donald is a fellow at the Manhattan Institute and contributing editor at the institute's City Journal. *In the following viewpoint, she responds to an article by former George W. Bush speechwriter Michael Gerson that supports amnesty for illegal immigrants. Mac Donald aims to explode what she considers the myth of Hispanic family values through an analysis of statistical data on Hispanic drop-out and illegitimacy rates.*

As you read, consider the following questions:

1. What is the Hispanic drop-out rate, as reported by Mac Donald?

2. According to the Department of Homeland Security, as cited by the author, what percentage of illegal immigrants may not qualify for the proposed amnesty because of their criminal records?

3. What percentage of Hispanic children are born out of wedlock, according to the author?

Heather Mac Donald, "Drop the N-Word Already," *National Review*, May 29, 2007. Reproduced by permission.

To observe the sentimental fantasy and ruthless political calculation that fuels the [George W.] Bush administration's immigration plans, one need only turn to Michael Gerson's most recent *Washington Post* column. Former Bush speechwriter Gerson was a powerful voice in the White House, especially on the matter of injecting faith into policy-making; his May 25 [2007] column provides a window into how the administration deals with facts.

Gerson accuses opponents of the Senate's recent amnesty proposal of a nativist fear of illegal immigrants. Such a fear, he argues, will hurt the Republican party's electoral chances and miss an opportunity to make the country even more religious. Powerlineblog.com's Paul Mirengoff has dismantled Gerson's key arguments, rejecting in particular his claim that illegal immigrants' religiosity should affect policy decisions about their fate: "The belief that matters most for purposes of this debate [writes Mirengoff] is not religious but civic—not belief in God but belief in our institutions and love for our country. It is the latter kind of thinking, and only such thinking, that will result in successful assimilation."

But Gerson's column is flawed on another front as well: It recycles open-borders bromides that have nothing to do with the truth. In warning against a rejection of amnesty, Gerson states: "If the Republican Party [GOP] cannot find ways to appeal to natural entrepreneurs, with strong family values, who are focused on education and social mobility, then the GOP is already dead."

The Myth of Latino Values

What planet is Gerson living on? Far from being "focused on education," Hispanics have the highest drop-out rate in the country—47 percent nationally, and far worse in heavily Hispanic areas. Schools in illegal-immigrant-saturated southern California spend enormous sums trying to persuade Latino students to stay in school and study, without avail. In the Los

Fertility in the Past Year, by Marital Status, Race and Ethnicity: 2008

	Women Giving Birth in the Past Year		
	All	Unmarried	Percent unmarried
Hispanic	936,020	396,019	42.3
Native born	453,583	231,848	51.1
Foreign born	482,437	164,171	34.0
White alone, not Hispanic	2,443,259	668,769	27.4
Black alone, not Hispanic	618,757	441,648	71.4
Asian alone, not Hispanic	231,583	29,085	12.6
Other, not Hispanic	124,348	64,992	52.3
Total	4,353,967	1,600,513	36.8

Note: "Unmarried" consists of divorced, separated, never married, and widowed.

TAKEN FROM: Pew Hispanic Center Tabulations of 2008 American Community Survey.

Angeles Unified School District, just 40 percent of Hispanics graduate, and those students who do finish school come out with abysmal skills. A controversial high school exit exam in California would require seniors to correctly answer just 51 percent of questions testing eighth-grade-level math and ninth-grade-level English in order to receive a diploma. Naturally, immigrant advocates have fiercely opposed this all-too-meager measure for school and student accountability. The California Research Bureau predicts that the exam will result in a Hispanic graduation rate of below 30 percent.

Behind Hispanic educational failure rate lies an apathy towards *learning*, as the Manhattan Institute's Herman Badillo argues in *One Nation, One Standard*. Hostility towards academic achievement is higher among Hispanics than among blacks. Factor in gang involvement and teenage pregnancy, and the Hispanic drop-out rate looks almost inevitable. The Department of Homeland Security estimates that a whopping 15 percent to 20 percent of illegal immigrants may not qualify for the proposed amnesty because of their criminal records, according to the *Wall Street Journal*. Gerson's claim of a culture "focused on education" is pure delusion.

Family Values?

Gerson's hackneyed invocation of Hispanic "family values" is equally laughable. Nearly 50 percent of all Hispanic children are born out of wedlock, compared to 24 percent of white children and 15 percent of Asian children. Black out-of-wedlock births are higher—68 percent—but the black population is not growing rapidly. And the fertility rate among unmarried Hispanic women is the highest in the country—over three times that of whites and Asians, and nearly one and a half times that of black women. The Hispanic teen-fertility rate also far outstrips other groups. Among Mexicans and Mexican-Americans, the teen birthrate is 93 births per every 1,000 girls, compared with 27 births for every 1,000 white girls, 17 births for every 1,000 Asian girls, and 65 births for every 1,000 black girls. As conservative policymakers such as Gerson should know, there is no better predictor of future social pathologies than out-of-wedlock childrearing.

Low levels of education and high levels of illegitimacy help explain why, contrary to Gerson's myths, Hispanics are not showing the "social mobility" of other immigrant groups past and present, as Harvard's George Borjas has documented and *City Journal's* Steve Malanga has reported.

Gerson's disregard for basic accuracy makes his Machiavellian [cunning or deceitful] view of the law all the more troubling. He claims that Republicans must do whatever it takes to capture a portion of the "fastest-growing segment of the electorate" (of course, what is growing fastest is the illegal population, who as of yet are not entitled to vote). "At one level," writes Gerson, "any immigration debate concerns a raw political calculation: Who ends up with more voters?" Such "raw political calculations" clearly govern White House machinations, but here are some factors that influence less partisan observers of the immigration mess: respect for the rule of law and a desire to show fairness to foreigners who comply with our immigration policies. In the American heartland, it is illegal aliens' disregard for U.S. immigration rules that most infuriates the public.

Periodical and Internet Sources Bibliography

The following articles have been selected to supplement the diverse views presented in this chapter.

Rebecca M. Cuevas de Caissie	"Hispanic Cultural Values: Family," *Bella Online*, 2010. www.bellaonline.com.
Ed Hooper	"Immigration Furor Blots Hispanic Achievement," *Atlanta Journal Constitution*, July 6, 2010.
Bob Menendez	"Latinos Have Made It, but There's Still Work to Be Done," CNN.com, October 19, 2009. http://articles.cnn.com.
Sarah Netter	"Who's to Blame for Marcello's Murder?" ABC.com, November 17, 2008. http://abcnews.go.com.
Mark Potok	"Anti-Latino Hate Crimes Rise for Fourth Year in a Row," *Southern Poverty Law Center*, October 29, 2008. www.splcenter.org.
Miguel A. Quiñones	"Getting More Hispanics to the Top," *Forbes.com*, August 23, 2010. www.forbes.com.
Walter Rodgers	"Illegal Hispanic Immigration Is Undermining American Values," *Christian Science Monitor*, March 30, 2010.
Mara Schiavocampo	"Anti-Latino Hate Crimes," MSNBC.com, September 2, 2009. http://dailynightly.msnbc.msn.com.
Washington Watcher	"In San Francisco, 'Hate Crime Hysteria' Metastasizes into 'Hate Speech' Totalitarianism," VDARE.com, August 25, 2009. www.vdare.com.
Guy White	"Hate Crimes: The Whitey Did It?" *Global Politician*, April 20, 2008.

CHAPTER 2

What Immigration Attitudes and Policies Affect the U.S. Latino Community?

Chapter Preface

In recent years, the issue of birthright citizenship has been thrust to the forefront of the contentious immigration reform debate. In the United States, the Constitution sets out the right of birthright citizenship in the Fourteenth Amendment, which states in its citizenship clause: "All persons born or naturalized in the United States, and subject to the jurisdiction thereof, are citizens of the United States and of the State wherein they reside." This means that any baby born in the country (including the territories of Puerto Rico, Guam, the US Virgin Islands, and the Northern Mariana Islands) is automatically a citizen of the United States, which is known in legal parlance as *jus soli*. Birthright citizenship is also granted to most children born to American parents overseas.

Anti-immigration forces, looking for ways to curb illegal immigration to the United States, turned their attention to the issue of birthright citizenship. In particular, they began to question the practice of granting automatic citizenship on a *jus soli* basis, arguing that undocumented immigrants were coming to the United States just to give birth to babies that would automatically have US citizenship. Anti-immigration leaders and politicians began to call these children "anchor babies," which quickly became a controversial term in the immigration debate. The activists who use this term mean it in a derogatory manner, implying that these babies will anchor their parents to the United States. They insinuate that *jus soli* citizenship encourages undocumented immigrants to come to the United States to have an anchor baby just to improve their chances of obtaining legal residency.

Anti-immigration politicians have introduced bills to circumvent the citizenship clause of the Fourteenth Amendment. These bills declare US-born children of foreign nationals exempt from the jurisdiction of the United States—and therefore, its Constitution. Such bills are designed to make sure citizenship is not granted unless at least one parent is a US citizen or lawful permanent resident. None of these bills has successfully passed through Congress.

Unsuccessful on that front, anti-immigration politicians began to propose that the citizenship clause could be changed through a constitutional amendment. On January 16, 2009, a US Senate resolution was introduced for that very reason. As of March 2011, Senate Joint Resolution 6 has not yet been approved by Congress for ratification by the states, and commentators believe that it will have an uphill battle.

Opponents of any such constitutional amendment or other legislation that would change the practice of *jus soli* citizenship argue that anti-immigration legislators are not only trying to eliminate birthright citizenship, but are also changing what it means to be an American. On August 11, 2010, conservative politician Linda Chavez stated that position very succinctly in the *Wall Street Journal*:

> Our history has been largely one of continuously expanding the community of people regarded as Americans, from native-born whites to freed slaves to Indians to naturalized citizens of all races and ethnicities. Since the abolition of slavery, we have never denied citizenship to any group of children born in the U.S.—even when we denied citizenship to their parents, as we did Asian immigrants from 1882 to 1943. This expansive view of who is an American has been critical to our successful assimilation of millions of newcomers.

The attempt to end birthright citizenship is one of the topics explored in the following chapter, which focuses on immigration and the Latino community. Other subjects debated include Arizona's immigration law, whether racism infected the debate over health-care reform, and whether undocumented immigrants increase crime rates.

> "[If] we critically examine the motives
> behind these anti-Latino laws, it's clear
> that many people in Arizona and be-
> yond fear and loathe the long-term
> consequence of Mexican immigration
> in particular and the demographic
> boom of Latinos in general, resulting in
> the browning of America."

Arizona's Immigration Law Is Racist

Alvaro Huerta

*Alvaro Huerta is a doctoral student at University of California,
Berkeley. In the following viewpoint, he criticizes two 2010 Arizona laws as racist: SB 1070, which requires police officers to demand legal documentation of an individual's immigration status; and HB 2281, which bans ethnic studies in public schools.
Huerta describes both laws as anti-Latino and argues that they
are based on fear of the increasingly powerful Latino demographic in Arizona.*

As you read, consider the following questions:

1. What historical figure does the author compare Arizona
   governor Jan Brewer to?

Alvaro Huerta, "Fear and Loathing of Mexicans," *Counterpunch*, June 11–13, 2010.
Reproduced by permission.

2. How did Barack Obama react to Brewer's signing of the immigration law, according to Huerta?

3. How do Brewer and Tom Horne rationalize the elimination of ethnic studies programs in public schools, in the author's opinion?

Not to be outdone [by] the late segregationist, Alabama Gov. George Wallace, Arizona Gov. Jan Brewer will go down in the history books as an ardent xenophobe and racist.

Brewer's hatred of immigrants and disregard for the civil rights of Latinos (both legal residents and citizens) have come to fruition in Arizona's recently [in 2010] passed laws aimed at criminalizing immigrants, racially profiling Latinos and denying racial minorities the right to learn about their history.

I'm speaking, of course, of SB 1070, the unconstitutional law that requires police officers to demand legal documentation of individuals suspected of being undocumented immigrants under the premise of "reasonable suspension" and HB 2281, the racist law that bans ethnic studies (optional courses, as a matter of fact) in public schools.

Stop Placating Racists

Instead of chastising Brewer for her racist legislative actions, President Barack Obama recently invited her to the White House to discuss the controversial immigration law that the president referred to as "misguided." This is the same president that had a "Beer Summit" at the White House with a racist police officer, Sgt. James Crowley, shortly after he arrested Harvard Professor Henry Louis Gates, Jr.—a distinguished African American scholar—in his own home. This high profile arrest can be traced to Gates' initial "inability" to verify proof of residence to Crowley even after Gates provided his Harvard faculty identification card.

As any parent should know, this is no way of rewarding bad behavior!

"Arizona's Illegal Employer Problem Solved!" Cartoon by Keith Tucker. www.Cartoon Stock.com.

Better yet, instead of meeting with Brewer in a one-to-one meeting usually afforded to world leaders, Obama should chastise the rogue governor and take direct action against Arizona's racist agenda. Obama can learn a thing or two from previous presidents. For instance, in 1963, then-President John F. Kennedy federalized the Alabama National Guard when Gov. Wallace attempted to prevent two African American students from attending the University of Alabama under a federal court order to desegregate public schools.

The Case of George Wallace

An ardent segregationist, Wallace, who operated under the political platform "segregation now, segregation tomorrow, segregation forever," eventually caved under pressure when confronted by the military might of the federal government. Taking this historical event as a "teachable moment," Obama needs to use all of his executive powers, including unmatch-

able oratory skills, to immediately repeal both SB 1070 and HB 2281. While Obama and U.S. Attorney General Eric Holder contemplate legal action, individuals of Mexican decent in this desert state live in a constant state of fear, anxiety and financial insecurity.

When she originally signed SB 1070 into law on April 23rd, Brewer assured the public that racial profiling would not be tolerated. However, what does she—a white, privileged politician—know about racial profiling? I wonder if she, or any member of her family, has even been a victim of racial profiling? More specifically, has she ever been denied a taxicab in the city of New York or other major city because of the color of her skin? Has she ever been pulled over by a police officer for simply being in the "wrong neighborhood" or because she allegedly "matched the description" of someone suspected of committing a crime?

While Brewer and the supporters of this anti-immigrant law attempt to frame this policy measure as one of "crime" and "safety," especially with the law's official name, "Support Our Law Enforcement and Safe Neighborhoods Act," they have yet to produce any hard data correlating immigration with crime in the state. There is a word in the dictionary for making false accusations: slander.

Other Racist Moves

While much of the attention in the media has been given to this cruel immigration law, Brewer wasted no time in attacking the Latino community, once again, with the elimination of ethnic studies programs in public schools.

In an Orwellian [totalitarian] maneuver, Brewer, the architect of this ban—Arizona's school chief Tom Horne—and other supporters argue that ethnic studies programs allegedly promote ethnic chauvinism, reverse racism against whites and the overthrow of the U.S. government. It is amazing how educational programs aimed at providing a more ethnically di-

verse interpretation of American life and history have now become eminent enemies of the state.

For instance, how is teaching a Latino high school student about the United Farm Workers (UFW) and the fact that Cesar Chavez was born in Yuma, Arizona, suddenly un-American? How is teaching a young Latina student about Dolores Huerta, the co-founder of the UFW, now a criminal act? Does this mean that Latino and Asian students can't learn about the unconscionable Japanese American internment camps, where the state of Arizona hosted one, during the mid-20th Century since this falls under the purview of "ethnic studies" programs? The only logical conclusion here is an obvious attempt by those in power to erase the history of discrimination and social injustice committed against racial minorities in the state and beyond.

Finally, if we critically examine the motives behind these anti-Latino laws, it's clear that many people in Arizona and beyond fear and loathe the long-term consequence of Mexican immigration in particular and the demographic boom of Latinos in general, resulting in the browning of America.

> "To say the law is racist is just inconsistent with both facts and intention."

Arizona's Immigration Law Is Not Racist

Bruce Maiman

Bruce Maiman is a radio talk show host and an opinion writer. In the following viewpoint, he argues that Arizona's 2010 immigration bill is not racist, because it does not target one particular race of people—it targets illegal immigrants. Moreover, he points out that racial profiling is against the law in Arizona, and law enforcement and government officials have made it quite clear that racial profiling would never be tolerated in the state. Editor's note: This article was written before the law was revised to accommodate charges brought in a lawsuit filed against Arizona by the US Department of Justice. Police agencies throughout the state initially opposed to certain provisions in the law reversed themselves and gave their support once those provisions were revised.

As you read, consider the following questions:

1. What percentage of illegal immigrants in Arizona come from Mexico, according to the author?

2. Does Maiman believe Arizona's immigration law can be abused?

3. What red flags does the author believe police will be on the lookout for in their search for illegal immigrants?

Since Arizona passed its controversial new immigration bill [in 2010], it's been nearly impossible to avoid charges by its opponents that the law is racist.

It's not racist.

That belief that it *is* racist is born out of what has become that law's most controversial of its several provisions: It gives police the power to question anyone they suspect might be in the country illegally. Immigrants' rights groups say that's racial profiling.

It's a bit irritating to hear that allegation. What do you mean it's profiling? They haven't started enforcing anything yet. Plenty of people in Arizona from the governor on down have made clear there will be no profiling nor will profiling be tolerated; it's against the law in Arizona, just as it was before the current immigration law was passed and just as it will continue to be illegal afterwards.

What the Law Says

To be racist, the law would have to specifically target one particular race of people. The law would have to specifically say that it is the intention of the legislature of Arizona for police to harass anyone of Latino heritage or brown skin.

That's not what the law says. The law is directed at illegal immigrants. It's only by dint of geographic circumstance that almost 100 percent of the illegal immigrants in Arizona come from Mexico.

If illegals in Arizona were Swedish or Mongolian, the law would apply to them.

Why is this so hard to apprehend: Arizona is a border state with Mexico. It's heavily impacted by illegal immigration.

There are nearly half a million illegal immigrants in a state with a relatively small population. They cause a problem for Arizona and Arizona wants to do something about that. I don't see anything in that line of reasoning that is racist. All of those things are legitimate concerns, are they not?

Vigilance Against Abuse

Could the law be abused? Of course it could. Any law can be abused. There's a possibility of abuse with every single law we've ever passed.

We act as if this law has some special quality about it that invites more abuse than some other law. Any law can be abused and any law enforcement officer can act like a jerk—or worse.

If a peace officer, in enforcing this law, indulges in clear racial profiling, violates the Fourth Amendment or goes beyond the intent or language of this law—they have to be disciplined, and if need be, prosecuted. That's not the law being racist but someone carrying out the law being racist by abusing it. It should go without saying that we have to be vigilant to insure the law isn't abused. Our legal system provides abundant recourse in which to conduct such vigilance. We can certainly be more vigilant about any abuse of immigration law than we've been about enforcing the immigration laws currently on the books—not that this would be saying much; we've done almost nothing to enforce the immigration laws currently on the books in this country.

Federal Government Failure

In fact, one of the reasons the Arizona legislature is trying to muscle its way out of its immigration problems on its own is because the federal government *has* dragged its feet on the matter of illegal immigration—so much so that it ignores cotton-headed sanctuary city policies in municipalities all across the country. These are policies that make no secret about their sanctuary laws, which tell their police departments *not* to enforce the federal immigration laws. Yet, the feds do nothing. That's part of what Arizona is reacting to.

Since 1986 when Congress passed the Simpson-Mazzoli Act, the federal government has failed in its responsibility to enforce its own law—looking the other way when employers knowingly hired illegals and treated them shabbily; knowingly looking the other way when the border was being compromised because it provided cheap labor.

So it's understandable why Arizona has reacted the way it has.

Arizona will have to police this law carefully to ensure that it is not abused, but it is not a racist law. Nor is the act of passing it a racist act. No one can bear the intellectual responsibility of that argument because that's not what the intent of the Arizona legislature was and that's quite clear. It is an immigration bill, not a brown people bill or a Mexican bill.

Law Enforcement Will Act Responsibly

Suggesting any intent of racial profiling isn't even in consonance with Arizona law enforcement groups which largely opposed the measure. They didn't want to be burdened with such an option, perhaps knowing full well that mistakes might be made, misunderstandings would occur and lawsuits would result. In other words, the police already were reticent about the law. Now that it's passed, they're even more likely to tread carefully.

Police officers in Arizona already have enough to do. They're not going to be out there looking for mothers taking their kids to school or motorists minding their business on the way to work.

In the normal course of their day, they'll keep a weather eye out for specific red flags—a van packed with individuals that has telltale signs of a coyote [a person who smuggles illegal immigrants into the country] situation; a motorist pulled over for running a stop sign who speaks no English, seems to have no license, doesn't seem to comprehend what's going on—that might be a tip off that someone is illegal.

But it's not like the police of Arizona have so much free time on their hands they're going to hassle citizens just for driving down the street.

Racist Individuals, Not Laws

To be sure, there will be instances of abuse and there will be bogus allegations of racism by someone who may not have liked that he got stopped because he had a busted tail light. But that has nothing to do with the intention of the law; it has to do with the actions of the individual. To say the law is racist is just inconsistent with both facts and intention. And it's unfair to Arizonans. It imputes to the state of Arizona some sort of mean-spiritedness. That's why some are now calling for economic boycotts of Arizona. The mayor of Phoenix plans to file a lawsuit against the state to block the law.

All Arizona is guilty of here is trying to deal with problems within its border, and trying to do so in a country in which the federal government has totally abandoned its responsibility to deal effectively with the subject of illegal immigration.

If you can show how this law is racist, or how the legislature of Arizona is racist, or how the people of Arizona are racist because they want to do something about the nearly half-million illegal immigrants in their state, which is costing them money and has caused crime to increase significantly— if you can explain how that gets to be racist, I'm fascinated to hear your logic.

| "Fear of 'the other'—of those who look or sound different, who come from poor countries with unfamiliar customs—has been at the heart of every immigration debate this country has ever had."

The Immigration Reform Debate Is Racist

Linda Chavez

Linda Chavez is an author and the chairman of the Center for Equal Opportunity. In the following viewpoint, she argues that many of the opponents of immigration are hardened xenophobes who are fearful of people who look or sound different from them—an unfortunate and recurring characteristic of the immigration debate since the founding of America. Chavez contends that America has struggled to overcome its prejudices and racial resentments and that the American people cannot let a group of prejudiced individuals derail the progress it has made over the centuries.

Linda Chavez, "Latino Fear and Loathing," Townhall.com, May 25, 2007. Reproduced by permission of Linda Chavez and Creators Syndicate, Inc.

As you read, consider the following questions:

1. What percentage of Americans does Chavez view as the core group of anti-immigrationists?

2. Who numbers among this group, to the author's dismay?

3. How many illegal aliens are living and working in America, according to Chavez?

Some people just don't like Mexicans—or anyone else from south of the border. They think Latinos are freeloaders and welfare cheats who are too lazy to learn English. They think Latinos have too many babies, and that Latino kids will dumb down our schools. They think Latinos are dirty, diseased, indolent and more prone to criminal behavior. They think Latinos are just too different from us ever to become real Americans.

No amount of hard, empirical evidence to the contrary, and no amount of reasoned argument or appeals to decency and fairness, will convince this small group of Americans—fewer than 10 percent of the general population, at most—otherwise. Unfortunately, among this group is a fair number of Republican members of Congress, almost all influential conservative talk radio hosts, some cable news anchors—most prominently, Lou Dobbs—and a handful of public policy "experts" at organizations such as the Center for Immigration Studies, the Federation for American Immigration Reform, NumbersUSA, in addition to fringe groups like the Minuteman Project.

The Core of the Debate

Stripped bare, this is what the current debate on immigration reform is all about. Fear of "the other"—of those who look or sound different, who come from poor countries with unfamiliar customs—has been at the heart of every immigration de-

Racism and Immigration

Perhaps the flare-up of the immigration issue started out more legitimately. Certainly there ere serious problems with waves of hundreds of thousands of people entering any country illegally. But like the head of a monstrous snake coming out of a thorny bush, the issue has grown its own nasty viper. Immigration has become the new magnet of American racism.

It's time to recognize this evil trend, and confront it.

Jose Barreiro,
Indian Country Today, *August 18, 2008.*

bate this country has ever had, from the infamous Alien and Sedition Acts of 1798 to the floor of the U.S. Senate this week [in May 2007].

What is said today of the Mexicans, Guatemalans, Salvadorans and others was once said of Germans, Swedes, the Irish, Italians, Poles, Jews and others. The only difference is that in the past, the xenophobes could speak freely, unconstrained by a veneer of political correctness. Today, they speak more cautiously, so they talk about the rule of law, national security, amnesty, whatever else they think might make their arguments less racially charged.

Where once the xenophobes could advocate forced sterilization and eugenics coupled with virtually shutting off legal immigration from "undesirable" countries, now they must be content with building walls, putting troops on the border, rounding up illegal aliens on the job and deporting them, passing local ordinances to signal their distaste for immigrants' multi-family living arrangements, and doing whatever else they can to drive these people back where they came from.

Xenophobes Will Not Win

There is no chance this small group of xenophobes will succeed—ultimately. The victories of their predecessors have been short-lived and so obviously wrong-headed we've always finally abandoned them, from modifying and then repealing the Asian exclusion acts to scrapping the nationalities quotas. But we need to quit pretending that the "No Amnesty" crowd is anything other than what it is: a tiny group of angry, frightened and prejudiced loudmouths backed by political opportunists who exploit them.

The status quo—largely turning a blind eye toward the 12 million illegal aliens who work, pay taxes and keep their noses clean, while stepping up border enforcement and selective internal enforcement—may not be the worst possible outcome in the current debate on immigration reform. It is the coward's way out of our current dilemma. But there are other problems with allowing the xenophobes to derail comprehensive immigration reform.

We've struggled long and hard as a nation to overcome our prejudices, enduring a Civil War and countless dead for the right to be judged by the content of our character not the color of our skin or where we came from. Our country is the greatest, freest, most powerful and optimistic nation in the history of the world—and our people are good, decent, fair and the hardest working anywhere. That is why immigrants— even those who look and sound different, from nearby and far away—come here, often with only the clothes on their backs but a fire in their bellies to succeed. They make all of us richer, and by embracing and welcoming them, we make ourselves better.

"The final refuge of pro-immigration sympathizers who cannot support their position with logic is racism."

Wanting to Limit Immigration Is Not Racist

Randy Alcorn

Randy Alcorn is a resident of Santa Barbara County, California. In the following viewpoint, he contends that it is not racist to observe that illegal immigrants are breaking the law and that illegal immigration has deleterious effects on border communities. Alcorn argues that illegal immigration is a serious problem that must be dealt with in order to protect the United States.

As you read, consider the following questions:

1. What does Alcorn list as the consequences of illegal immigration?

2. How does Alcorn respond to the pro-immigration argument that immigrants are just hard-working people trying to support their families?

3. According to the author, what was the result of the 1986 amnesty?

Randy Alcorn, "Idiocies in Illegal Immigrant Debate," *Santa Maria Times*, May 23, 2010. Reproduced by permission of the author.

Arizona and California, along with other southwestern states, are taking the brunt of a relentless assault of illegal immigration that is spreading across the country.

It is diluting public education, straining welfare programs, bankrupting hospitals, increasing violent crime, overcrowding prisons, eroding pay scales of manual labor jobs, putting more unlicensed and uninsured drivers on our highways—and is virtually the sole source of America's disturbing, Third World rate of population growth.

An Insidious Problem

Illegal immigration has been left untreated too long. It is a serious ailment for America. Arizona's controversial remedy is born of desperation, but not entirely unprecedented.

Policing is a necessary evil most of us resent. If we drive a car at night, we are subjected to arbitrary sobriety stops. If we travel by air, we must endure personally intrusive security screening at airports.

In both cases, we must produce ID to prove who we are. Because some people drive drunk and some people blow up airplanes, we grudgingly accept these police intrusions.

Because Arizona is being overwhelmed by illegal aliens, state law now allows police to demand proof of legal residency, but only in a lawful stop, detention or arrest. Nevertheless, that law is another irksome, police-state intrusion imposed on us because of a criminal minority.

Idiotic Rationalizations

Some people, including police, are refusing to abide by the Arizona law. What is it about illegal immigration that defies common sense among so many people?

If, as the TV character Dr. House is fond of saying, "most people are idiots," few issues confronting America today more starkly reveal that disturbing possibility than does the issue of illegal immigration.

Perhaps the most repeated idiotic rationalization for tolerating the invasion of foreign trespassers is that they are just hard-working people trying to support their families.

The fact that they broke our laws to be here is somehow excused by their irresponsibly having children they couldn't support in their native land. Extending this rationale, we could forgive bank robbers, burglars and tax cheats who have families to support.

If the need to support a family earns one a free pass to America, we had better be prepared for a tidal wave of immigrants. The world has millions of families just a missed meal away from starvation.

Too much charity is not a virtue. Our national resources have limits. We ignore this reality at our own peril. After the locusts of human overpopulation ravage America, what will be left for Earth's hordes to devour?

A Nation of Immigrants?

The next illogical argument is that we are a nation of immigrants—as if that cliché somehow justifies illegal immigration. Are we, today, a nation of immigrants? If so, wouldn't that mean that most Americans alive today were born in a country other than America, to parents who were not Americans?

Go back far enough into history, and you will find that most nations could claim to be a nation of immigrants. So what?

Amnesty as a Humane Act

Another pro-immigration argument that relies on emotion rather than on reason proposes that because they are here anyhow, illegal immigrants should be allowed to stay. Some have established themselves here, have families with children who, under a contorted interpretation of the Constitution, are automatic citizens. It would be inhumane to expel the trespassers now.

Prison is inhumane too, but a necessary consequence of unlawful behavior. Without consequences, there is no discipline. Without discipline there is no order. Without order there is no civilization.

There is no statute of limitations on international trespassing that allows one to become a legal permanent resident simply by avoiding deportation long enough. Didn't we try something like that back in 1986, by granting comprehensive amnesty? What did that get us but millions more trespassers?

The Canard of Racism

The final refuge of pro-immigration sympathizers who cannot support their position with logic is racism. The primitive reasoning here is that since most illegal immigrants are Hispanic, those who oppose illegal immigration must be racists.

This canard has been so overused that it has virtually lost all its power to shame, embarrass or scare anyone. But let's pretend for a moment that it is true. What would it change? Would all the deleterious consequences of illegal immigration go away simply because those who opposed it were racists?

Let's not be idiots.

> *"Nearly 60 percent of Latino gangs are illegal aliens, and the number of Latino gangs is increasing nationally."*

Undocumented Latino Immigrants Increase U.S. Crime Rates

Barbara Simpson

Barbara Simpson is a radio talk show host in San Francisco. In the following viewpoint, she asserts that America's long-standing generosity to immigrants has had deleterious consequences to American economic and social stability because of criminal gangs and the draining of social programs. Simpson also notes that there are political consequences, as she believes Latinos are being courted by Democrats in order to dominate national politics and impose one-party rule.

As you read, consider the following questions:

1. According to the author, why does President Obama want to provide amnesty for illegal aliens?

2. How many illegal aliens does Simpson say the government claims are in the United States?

Barbara Simpson, "Come on in—What's Mine Is Yours," WorldNetDaily.com, March 15, 2010. Reproduced by permission.

3. How many illegal aliens do border officials say are in the United States, according to the author?

H eads up, folks!

If you think the [Barack] Obama administration and his lapdog Congress put on the full-court press concerning the health-care legislation ... just wait a week and you'll see the same tactics, only worse, to push through a new immigration policy.

The president wants the proposal submitted by March 21 [2010—i.e., in less than a week]!

The Need for Reform

Barack Obama repeatedly says he'll keep his campaign promise to revise U.S. immigration laws, calling it "comprehensive immigration reform."

That sounds nice, but the real issue isn't just "immigration," it's *rampant illegal immigration.*

It's gone on for decades and increased dramatically as foreigners realized how easy it was to get in and stay in the United States and actually have the government take care of them.

Nice work if you can get it—and they can.

Some people say it doesn't matter. They like the mix of cultures. Others say the country needs illegals to do the jobs Americans won't do.

Tell that to long-term unemployed citizens whose savings have run out.

Obama counts heavily on the Hispanic vote and uses the political clout of organizations such as [National Council of] La Raza and MALDEF [Mexican American Legal Defense and Educational Fund], as well as union pressure, to ram through whatever he wants. The administration meets regularly with such organizations pulling together their plans.

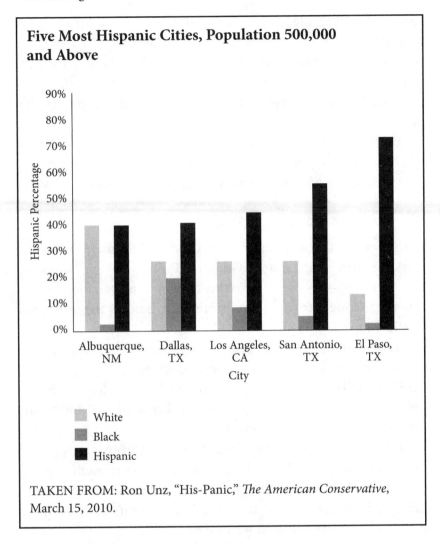

Five Most Hispanic Cities, Population 500,000 and Above

TAKEN FROM: Ron Unz, "His-Panic," *The American Conservative*, March 15, 2010.

Obama Wants Amnesty

Regardless of the window-dressing the Washington mafia puts on it, the bottom line is that Obama and the mob want to legalize illegal aliens.

Whether called "amnesty" or a "pathway to citizenship," there's no difference. It would reward with citizenship people who sneak across our borders, spread into every state, take low-paying jobs undercutting American workers, often getting paid under the table, using fake or stolen Social Security numbers, paying little or no taxes and draining our social welfare, educational, medical, law enforcement, judicial and other services.

Logic? None, except that for Obama and the others, it's politics as usual.

Bottom line, it's seen as assuring Democrats a solid block of Hispanic votes in any election on any level—for decades.

If you don't like the one-party rule we have now, just wait!

The Pathway to Citizenship

But it's not only Democrats. Sen. Charles Schumer, D-N.Y., is working with Sen. Lindsey Graham, R-S.C.—at the behest of the president—to come up with a plan that can be quickly moved through to passage, preferably before the midterm elections!

Their "immigrant blueprint" will involve "pathway" plus a temporary-worker program, some kind of "tamperproof ID card" for citizens—meaning a national ID card for citizens—border surveillance to prevent further illegal entries and whatever other goodies they jam in.

But there's a basic problem. They can't even get together on the number of illegals here now. The government says 10 million to 12 million. Border officials, law enforcement and others who've monitored the situation for years say the figure is between 30 million and 40 million.

What do you think would happen to local and state budgets if all those people suddenly were "legal" with a blank check to public coffers?

Average Americans already face the impact of illegals on their lives, schools and communities every day.

They pay the taxes that support the welfare programs that support the illegals.

They're people losing their houses and jobs and can't replace either while illegals get benefits and work unimpeded.

Social and Economic Effects

Facts and figures provided by law enforcement, schools, social-welfare departments, medical facilities and social scientists show that illegal aliens have caused massive social upheaval, escalating law-enforcement problems including rising crime rates, a strain on local, county and state budgets across the country and a not-yet-admitted impact on rising national unemployment.

They are responsible for serious crime involving dangerous gangs dealing drugs and worse. The *Los Angeles Times* reported that nearly 60 percent of Latino gangs are illegal aliens, and the number of Latino gangs is increasing nationally.

On Friday [in March 2010], 26 members of the violent gang MS-13 were charged with racketeering, murder, attempted murder, kidnapping and robbery in metropolitan Atlanta. Many of those gang members are illegal aliens, and there are MS-13 gangs in almost every state.

Despite the crimes, politically correct politicians forbid "profiling" or residency inquiries of suspects, and "sanctuary cities" protect criminal illegals, leaving honest citizens at their mercy.

Generosity Is Hurting the Country

The U.S. has provided asylum to millions and welcomed immigrants from across the planet. Unfortunately, our generosity now exceeds common sense and logic.

We're suffering financially, socially and culturally and society is fraying at the edges while our ostensible leaders dig in their heels and refuse to change their views because of PC politics.

If Barack Obama thinks he had problems with health care, he's in for a surprise when he latches onto immigration reform.

His March 21 deadline is also the date for *anti-reform* Americans to inundate the capital switchboard with calls and faxes to elected officials telling them *not* to push through that legislation. A march on Washington is also possible.

Demand Accountability

Loyal Americans got their message to Congress in 2007 when amnesty was attempted. As TV news showed angry, demonstrating illegals waving Mexican flags, American citizens got the message: their country was at stake.

The next time illegals march for "their rights," they'll wave American flags so citizens won't think they're anti-U.S.

It's just a tactic to fool us.

If people want to become Americans or want to work here, they should follow the law and the rules.

But spitting in our face and expecting to be rewarded is wrong, and any politician who defends that needs to be shown the door—from the president on down.

Remember that on Election Day—every Election Day.

I *"Hispanics have approximately the same crime rates as whites of the same age."*

Undocumented Latino Immigrants Do Not Increase U.S. Crime Rates

Ron Unz

Ron Unz is the publisher of the American Conservative. *In the following viewpoint, he questions whether media reports of increasing numbers of Hispanic crimes are overblown and analyzes FBI crime statistics to learn that Hispanics have approximately the same crime rates as whites. Unz concedes that there are reasonable concerns about Hispanic immigration, but mischaracterizing Hispanic crime rates will discredit anti-immigration arguments in the long run.*

As you read, consider the following questions:

1. What two factors does Unz identify as influencing the perception of the Hispanic crime rate?

2. What is the median age for Hispanics in America, according to the author?

Ron Unz, "His-Panic," *The American Spectator*, March 1, 2010. Reproduced by permission.

3. After adjusting for age, how do Hispanic incarceration rates compare to the white average, as reported by Unz?

According to [conservative commentator] Lou Dobbs, "a third of the prison population in this country is estimated to be illegal aliens," and [conservative commentator] Glenn Beck regularly warns of "an illegal alien crime wave." Congressman Tom Tancredo insists, "The face of illegal immigration on our borders is one of murder, one of drug smuggling, one of vandalism for all the communities along the border, and one of infiltration of people coming into this country for purposes to do us great harm." [Conservative commentator] Michelle Malkin adds an even more terrifying note, calling our borders "open channels not only for illegal aliens and drug smugglers, but terrorists, too." Even as far back as 2000, the highly regarded General Social Survey found that 73 percent of Americans believed that immigration caused higher crime rates, a level of concern considerably greater than fears about job losses or social unity.

Misperception of Immigrants

As Latino gangs have gained notoriety in the United States—particularly MS-13, dubbed the "The World's Most Dangerous Gang" by usually restrained *National Geographic*—images of violent foreigners have come to dominate much of the national debate on immigration policy. A perception has taken root in the minds of the American public and many elected leaders that the greatest threat posed by mass immigration is crime.

In recent decades, most immigrants have been Hispanic; Asians, who constitute the other large portion of the inflow, are generally regarded as economically successful and law-abiding. Although many Hispanics are American-born, the vast majority still comes from a relatively recent immigrant background. So to a considerable extent, popular concerns about immigrant crime and popular concerns about Hispanic crime amount to the same thing. While fears of perceived racial insensitivity may force many critics to choose their words carefully, widespread belief that Hispanics have high or perhaps very high crime rates seems to exist.

But is this correct? Or are these concerns rooted in the same excitable and ideological mindset that produced endless stories of Saddam [Hussein's] notorious WMD [weapons of mass destruction] with activists and their media accomplices passing along rumors and personal beliefs in pursuit of a political agenda rather than bothering to determine the facts? Does America face a Hispanic crime problem or merely a Hispanic crime hoax?

A Hispanic Crime Hoax

Personal experiences are no substitute for detailed investigation, but they sometimes provide a useful reality check. Since the early 1990s, I've lived in Silicon Valley, a region in which people of white European ancestry are a relatively small minority, separately outnumbered by both Asians and Hispanics, with many of the latter quite poor and often here illegally. On any given day, more than half of the people I encounter in Palo Alto are Hispanics from immigrant backgrounds. Yet my area of the country has exceptionally low crime rates and virtually no serious ethnic conflict. This confounds the expectations of many of my East Coast friends.

Prior to moving back to my native California, I lived for five years in Jackson Heights, Queens, one of the most heavily immigrant and ethnically diverse parts of New York City. There as well, white Europeans were a small minority and immigrants from various Latin American countries were the largest ethnic group, close to an absolute majority of the local population. On a typical afternoon or evening, probably 80 percent of the people walking the streets of my neighborhood were non-white, and on dozens of occasions I returned home from Manhattan on a late-night train, the only white face in the subway car. Yet in all my years of living there, I never encountered a hostile or menacing situation, let alone suffered an actual criminal attack. Hardly what one would expect from television images, let alone the wild claims made by conservative magazines or talk radio. The "thousands of brutal assailants and terrorists" *City Journal*'s Heather Mac Donald finds among our immigrant population must have moved into someone else's neighborhood.

So were my personal experiences atypical? Or are the media and conservative movement portrayals so completely wrong? Hispanics will constitute a quarter of the American population within a generation or two, according to current demographic projections, so this is an important issue for the future of our country.

Analyzing the Statistics

The obvious way to answer the question is to consult the public FBI Uniform Crime Report database, which provides aggregated information on the race of all criminal suspects throughout America. Unfortunately, there's a problem: Hispanic criminals are sometimes reported as "white" and sometimes not, rendering the federal crime data almost useless. Therefore, indirect means must be used to estimate the crime rate of Hispanics compared to whites. (Throughout this essay, "white" shall refer to non-Hispanic whites.)

One metric to examine might be relative incarceration rates, since most people who begin a life of criminal activity end up behind bars sooner or later—usually sooner. Furthermore, since so much of prison violence is along racial lines, correctional authorities are careful to record the ethnicity of individual inmates, and the aggregate data is made available annually by the Bureau of Justice Statistics [BJS]. Indeed, over the years, prison-reform groups such as The Sentencing Project, as well as various federal judges, have used this official

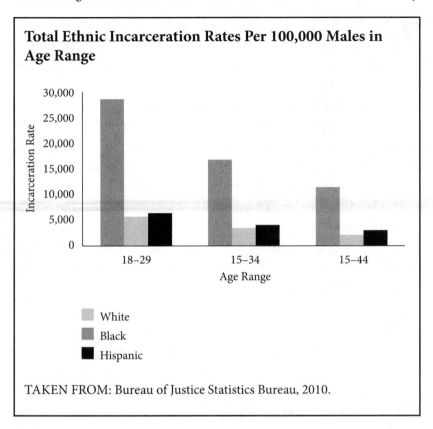

Total Ethnic Incarceration Rates Per 100,000 Males in Age Range

TAKEN FROM: Bureau of Justice Statistics Bureau, 2010.

data to criticize the prison system for its massive overrepresentation of racial minorities among inmates relative to their share of the population.

If we examine the data in the most recent 2008 BJS report, published in December 2009, we discover the total Hispanic incarceration rate, while far below that of blacks, is still almost 150 percent above the white average, having fallen a little from the 170 percent figure in 2000. So perhaps those fearful commentators are right and Hispanics commit crimes at roughly two-and-a-half times the rate of whites in America.

The traditional liberal explanation for this would be that Hispanics are considerably poorer than whites, that poverty and racism cause crime, and that a white-dominated criminal justice system is likely to be biased against suspects of a darker hue. There may or may not be some truth in these common liberal arguments, but since the name of this magazine is *The American Conservative*, let us put them aside at least for now and consider other possible factors.

The most obvious of these are age and gender. An overwhelming fraction of serious crime is committed by the young; young males in particular. This has been the case throughout recorded history and remains true everywhere in today's world. Almost all American crimes are committed by individuals aged 15–44, with the age range 18–29 representing the sharp peak of criminal activity. Also, the 14-to-1 ratio of males to females in the U.S. prison system provides a sense of just how heavily crime is a male phenomenon; for violent offenses, the ratio is even higher.

Focus on Age Distribution

And as it happens, the age distribution in America for Hispanics and non-Hispanic whites is quite different. The median age for Hispanics is around 27, near the absolute peak of the prime-crime age range. But the median white age is over 40, putting nearly half the white population above the likely age range for committing crimes. While it is certainly true that Hispanic 23-year-olds have much greater criminal tendencies than white 45-year-olds, a more useful question is the relative criminality of Hispanics and whites of the same age. Also, many Hispanics are immigrants, and since immigrants are more likely to be male, there will be a gender skew in the general Hispanic population. Therefore, let us consider the Hispanic imprisonment rate relative to the number of males in the high-crime age range.

Suddenly the numbers change quite a bit, with the relative Hispanic-to-white total incarceration rate dropping by a third or more for several of the age cohorts [statistical groups]. But even these lower figures may still be a bit misleading. As a recent front page *New York Times* story pointed out, over half of all federal prosecutions these days are for immigration-related offenses, and since a huge fraction of illegal immigrants are from south of the border, the 10 percent or so of U.S. prison inmates who are in federal custody might significantly distort our ethnic imprisonment statistics. Anyway, offenses such as robbery, rape, murder, burglary, assault, and theft are almost always prosecuted in state courts, so it makes sense to separate these street crimes from cases of illegal nannies convicted of illegal nannying.

Another important reason to focus on state-level imprisonment data is the evidence of vast differences among regional criminal-justice systems due to various cultural and political factors. For example, whites in Oklahoma are incarcerated at a rate almost 300 percent higher than whites in New Jersey, and while some of this disparity may result from the greater criminal tendencies of white Oklahomans, it seems likely that the harshness of the local courts and sentencing guidelines may also play an important role. We should therefore try to compare Hispanic incarceration rates with those for whites on a state-by-state basis so as to minimize the impact of differences in local criminal-justice systems.

The most recent BJS publications do not provide state-by-state incarceration data broken down by ethnicity, but the 2005 BJS Bulletin did exactly that, and while relative Hispanic incarceration rates have fallen somewhat in the past five years, the drop has not been large. Therefore, we should be able to use the 2005 figures with confidence.

Adjusting for Age

Our first discovery is that even before adjusting for age, the overall Hispanic incarceration rate drops from 150 percent above the white rate down to just 80 percent above, presumably reflecting the exclusion of immigration-related federal offenses. We can now use census data to estimate the number of prime-crime-age young males in the two groups, and since there is some uncertainty in deciding which age range is most appropriate for normalization purposes, we should probably explore the results with several different choices, such as 18–29, 15–34, and 15–44.5 (Many observers believe that the number of Hispanic illegal immigrants in America is sharply underestimated by the government; if so, this would correspondingly reduce the relative Hispanic imprisonment rate.)

The overall age-adjusted national imprisonment rates are shown in [the chart accompanying this viewpoint]. Hispanic incarceration rates are now between 13 and 31 percent above the white average, depending upon which age range we choose for normalization purposes. By contrast, the claims of extremely high relative black incarceration rates widely publicized several years ago by The Sentencing Project remain correct even after these age adjustment. . . .

The Real Crime Rates

The evidence presented here powerfully refutes the widespread popular belief that America's Hispanics have high crime rates. Instead, their criminality seems to fall near the center of the white national distribution, being somewhat higher than white New Englanders but somewhat lower than white Southerners. Taken as a whole, the mass of statistical evidence constitutes strong support for the "null hypothesis," namely that Hispanics have approximately the same crime rates as whites of the same age.

We must bear in mind that most Hispanics are still of very recent immigrant origins and thus are considerably poorer than the average American. There actually does exist a connection between poverty and crime, even if liberals make such a claim, and since today's Hispanic population has roughly the same crime rate as far more affluent whites, there is every reason to expect that this crime rate will drop further as Hispanics continue to move up the economic ladder. As the American Enterprise Institute's Douglas Besharov pointed out in an important but insufficiently noticed October 2007 *New York Times* column, the last decade or two have seen an extremely rapid economic advance for most of America's Hispanic population. This rise may be connected with the simultaneous and unexpectedly rapid drop in urban crime rates throughout the country.

Meanwhile, the national debate over immigration remains contentious. Restrictionists can provide numerous completely legitimate arguments in favor of their position, ranging from economic competition and cultural conflict to national overpopulation and environmental degradation. But they will discredit these by including unsubstantiated claims about crime. Conservatives have traditionally prided themselves on being realists, dealing with the world as it is rather than attempting to force it to conform to a pre-existing ideological framework. But just as many on the Right succumbed to a fantastical foreign policy that makes the world much more dangerous than it needs to be, some have also accepted the myth that Hispanic immigrants and their children have high crime rates. Such an argument may have considerable emotional appeal, but there is very little hard evidence behind it.

> "There is no constitutional impediment to Congress ending the granting of birthright citizenship to those whose presence here is 'not only without the government's consent but in violation of its law.'"

Birthright Citizenship Should Be Outlawed

George Will

George Will is a conservative syndicated columnist. In the following viewpoint, he observes that a simple reform would end the process of birthright citizenship—that a baby born to an illegal immigrant is automatically an American citizen—and bring the interpretation of the Fourteenth Amendment of the US Constitution more in line with what the law intended. Will argues that by interpreting the language of the citizenship clause logically, lawmakers can end the process of birthright citizenship, which would remove an incentive for illegal immigration.

As you read, consider the following questions:

1. When was the Fourteenth Amendment ratified, as reported by Will?

George Will, "An Argument to Be Made About Immigrant Babies and Citizenship," *Washington Post*, March 28, 2005. Reprinted with permission.

2. What percentage of births in Los Angeles are to mothers who are in the United States illegally, according to recent congressional testimony, as cited by the author?

3. According to congressional testimony, as reported by Will, what percentage of births in the United States are to mothers in the country illegally?

A simple reform would drain some scalding steam from immigration arguments that may soon again be at a roiling boil. It would bring the interpretation of the 14th Amendment into conformity with what the authors of its text intended, and with common sense, thereby removing an incentive for illegal immigration.

To end the practice of "birthright citizenship," all that is required is to correct the misinterpretation of that amendment's first sentence: "All persons born or naturalized in the United States, and subject to the jurisdiction thereof, are citizens of the United States and of the state wherein they reside." From these words has flowed the practice of conferring citizenship on children born here to illegal immigrants.

A parent from a poor country, writes professor Lino Graglia of the University of Texas law school, "can hardly do more for a child than make him or her an American citizen, entitled to all the advantages of the American welfare state." Therefore, "It is difficult to imagine a more irrational and self-defeating legal system than one which makes unauthorized entry into this country a criminal offense and simultaneously provides perhaps the greatest possible inducement to illegal entry."

Writing in the *Texas Review of Law and Politics*, Graglia says this irrationality is rooted in a misunderstanding of the phrase "subject to the jurisdiction thereof." What was this intended or understood to mean by those who wrote it in 1866 and ratified it in 1868? The authors and ratifiers could not have intended birthright citizenship for illegal immigrants because in 1868 *there were and never had been any illegal immigrants* because *no law ever had restricted immigration.*

What Would the Founders Think?

If those who wrote and ratified the 14th Amendment *had* imagined laws restricting immigration—and had anticipated huge waves of illegal immigration—is it reasonable to presume they would have wanted to provide the reward of citizenship to the children of the violators of those laws? Surely not.

The Civil Rights Act of 1866 begins with language from which the 14th Amendment's citizenship clause is derived: "All persons born in the United States, *and not subject to any foreign power*, excluding Indians not taxed, are hereby declared to be citizens of the United States." (Emphasis added.) The explicit exclusion of Indians from birthright citizenship was not repeated in the 14th Amendment because it was considered unnecessary. Although Indians were at least partially subject to U.S. jurisdiction, they owed allegiance to their tribes, not the United States. This reasoning—divided allegiance—applies equally to exclude the children of resident aliens, legal as well as illegal, from birthright citizenship. Indeed, today's regulations issued by the departments of Homeland Security and Justice stipulate:

> A person born in the United States to a foreign diplomatic officer accredited to the United States, as a matter of international law, is not subject to the jurisdiction of the United States. That person is not a United States citizen under the 14th Amendment.

Sen. Lyman Trumbull of Illinois was, Graglia writes, one of two "principal authors of the citizenship clauses in 1866 act and the 14th Amendment." He said that "subject to the jurisdiction of the United States" meant subject to its "complete" jurisdiction, meaning "not owing allegiance to anybody else."

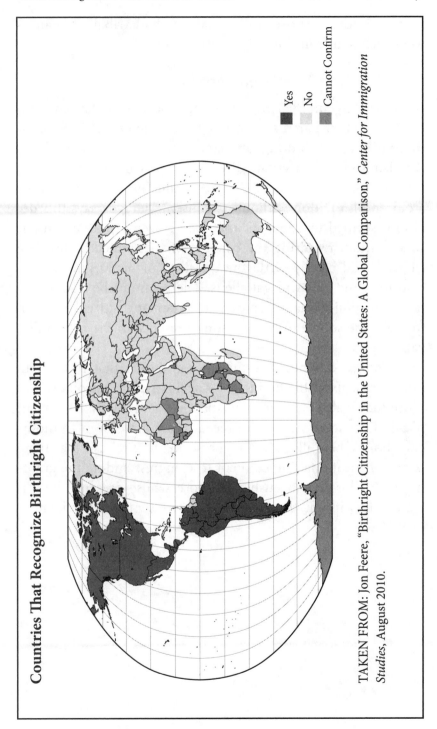

Countries That Recognize Birthright Citizenship

Yes
No
Cannot Confirm

TAKEN FROM: Jon Feere, "Birthright Citizenship in the United States: A Global Comparison," *Center for Immigration Studies*, August 2010.

Hence children whose Indian parents had tribal allegiances were excluded from birthright citizenship.

The Question Has Been Settled

Appropriately, in 1884 the Supreme Court held that children born to Indian parents were not born "subject to" U.S. jurisdiction because, among other reasons, the person so born could not change his status by his "own will without the action or assènt of the United States." And "no one can become a citizen of a nation without its consent." Graglia says this decision "seemed to establish" that U.S. citizenship is "a consensual relation, requiring the consent of the United States." So: "This would clearly settle the question of birthright citizenship for children of illegal aliens. There cannot be a more total or forceful denial of consent to a person's citizenship than to make the source of that person's presence in the nation illegal."

Congress has heard testimony estimating that more than two-thirds of all births in Los Angeles public hospitals, and more than half of all births in that city, and nearly 10 percent of all births in the nation in recent years, have been to mothers who are here illegally. Graglia seems to establish that there is no constitutional impediment to Congress ending the granting of birthright citizenship to those whose presence here is "not only without the government's consent but in violation of its law."

> "Birthright citizenship remains an eloquent statement about the nature of our society and a powerful force for immigrant assimilation."

Birthright Citizenship Should Not Be Outlawed

Eric Foner

Eric Foner is an author and a professor of history at Columbia University. In the following viewpoint, he traces the debate over US citizenship, which stretches back to the founding of the country and was transformed during the Civil War. Foner argues that the American concept of birthright citizenship makes a powerful statement about the inclusive nature of US society and sets the United States apart from the broad majority of nations around the world.

As you read, consider the following questions:

1. When was the first naturalization law enacted in the United States, according to the author?

2. How does Foner believe the Civil War transformed the debate over citizenship?

3. What year was immigration from countries in the Western Hemisphere limited, as reported by the author?

For almost 150 years Americans have believed that anyone born here, whatever his or her origins, can be a good citizen. There is no reason to believe the children of illegal immigrants are any different.

Congress should think long and hard before tampering with this essential American principle embodied in the 14th Amendment to the U.S. Constitution. Approved by Congress in 1866 at the outset of Reconstruction and ratified two years later, the amendment establishes the principle of birthright citizenship. With minor exceptions, all persons born in this country are American citizens, whatever the status of their parents.

Republican Lindsey Graham of South Carolina, several of his Senate colleagues and a number of conservative political commentators are now demanding that the amendment be reinterpreted or rewritten so as to exclude the children of illegal immigrants.

Bitter conflicts about who should be an American citizen are hardly new, nor are efforts to exclude those deemed for one reason or another undesirable. The very first naturalization law, enacted in 1790, barred non-white immigrants from ever becoming citizens. This prohibition was lifted for Africans in 1870 but lasted into the mid-20th century for Asians. In 1857, in the *Dred Scott* decision, Chief Justice Roger B. Taney declared that no black person, free or slave, could be a citizen of the U.S.

Union's Triumph

The Civil War transformed the debate over citizenship. In a sense, the 14th Amendment wrote into the Constitution the results of the Union's triumph and the destruction of slavery. It begins by defining as citizens all persons born or naturalized in the U.S. "and subject to the jurisdiction thereof"—language meant to exclude Indians, deemed to be citizens of their respective tribes, and American-born children of foreign diplomats. It goes on to bar states from depriving these citizens of life, liberty or property or denying them the "equal protection of the laws."

The most important change in the Constitution since the Bill of Rights, the 14th Amendment was intended, first, to establish beyond doubt the citizenship of the 4 million emancipated slaves and to consign *Dred Scott* to oblivion.

But the Republicans who controlled Congress also had a larger purpose. "It is a singular fact," the abolitionist Wendell Phillips wrote in 1866, "that, unlike all other nations, this nation has yet a question as to what makes or constitutes a citizen." The 14th Amendment established the first national definition of citizenship and with it the idea that these citizens enjoyed their rights as part of the American people rather than as members of particular racial or ethnic groups.

National Consciousness

In this, it reflected the expansion of national consciousness brought on by the Civil War. The struggle against slavery crystallized the idea of the national government as "the custodian of freedom," in the words of Massachusetts Senator Charles Sumner. The Black Codes enacted by all-white southern governments soon after the end of the war, which sought to reduce freed people to a condition reminiscent of slavery, reinforced the conviction that the states couldn't be trusted to respect Americans' basic rights.

Did Congress intend birthright citizenship to apply to the children of illegal residents? No such group existed in 1866; at the time, just about anyone who wished to enter the U.S. was free to do so. Only later were certain groups singled out for exclusion—prostitutes, polygamists, lunatics, anarchists, and, starting in 1882, the entire population of China.

Not until 1924 was the Border Patrol established, in connection with the law setting nationality quotas for immigration. Initially, its purpose was to keep "undesirable" Europeans—Italians, Greeks, and other southern Europeans—from sneaking across the Mexican border.

No Limits

Until 1965, there were no numerical limits on immigration from countries in the Western Hemisphere, so the issue of illegal Mexican immigrants, which so alarms today's critics of the 14th Amendment, didn't arise.

The closest analogy in 1866 to today's illegal aliens were immigrants from Asia, forever barred from American citizenship. The Chinese aroused considerable hostility among white Americans, especially on the West Coast, and with an eye on congressional elections, the amendment's opponents charged that it would make citizens of Chinese children born in this country. The amendment's authors didn't retreat in the face of blatant racism. They chose their words carefully; when they wrote "all persons," they meant it.

Universal Application

The Supreme Court has consistently ruled that birthright citizenship applies to every American-born child and equal protection of the laws to citizens and non-citizens alike. The key cases, decided in the late 19th century, were *U.S. v. Wong Kim Ark*, which affirmed the citizenship of children born to Chinese immigrants, and *Yick Wo v. Hopkins*, which overturned a San Francisco law discriminating against Chinese-owned laundries.

The juxtaposition of the 14th Amendment with the bar on the naturalization of Asian immigrants long affected Asian-American life. In the early 20th century, California barred aliens ineligible for citizenship from owning land, so Asian parents transferred title to their homes and farms to their citizen children. Not until World War II was China given a quota (all of 105 persons per year) of immigrants eligible for naturalization. Only with the immigration reform of 1965 did Asians achieve the same status as other immigrants.

"For Mankind"

The 14th Amendment made the Constitution what it is today: a document that guarantees the equal rights of all Americans and to which individuals and groups who feel they are being denied equality can appeal. As the 19th-century Republican editor George William Curtis wrote, it was part of a process that changed the U.S. government from one "for white men" to one "for mankind."

To be sure, as far as blacks were concerned the amendment fell into abeyance after the abandonment of Reconstruction. It was reinvigorated in the civil-rights era. Even today's conservative Supreme Court has used it to expand the rights of aggrieved Americans, as it did in *Lawrence v. Texas*, which in 2003 overturned a state law criminalizing homosexual acts.

Adopted as part of the effort to purge the nation of the legacy of slavery, birthright citizenship remains an eloquent statement about the nature of our society and a powerful force for immigrant assimilation. In a world where most countries limit access to citizenship via ethnicity, culture or religion, it sets our nation apart.

Periodical and Internet Sources Bibliography

The following articles have been selected to supplement the diverse views presented in this chapter.

Steve Chapman	"Immigration and Crime," *Reason*, February 22, 2010.
Ann Coulter	"Look Who's 'Nativist' Now," Townhall.com, August 18, 2010. http://townhall.com.
Phil Gingrey	"End Birthright Citizenship," *Hill*, September 2, 2010.
Virgil Goode	"End Birthright Citizenship," *Human Events*, July 22, 2010.
Daniel Griswold	"Unfounded Fear of Immigrant Crime Grips Arizona," *Washington Times*, May 25, 2010.
Barbara Simpson	"Adios, Baby!" WorldNetDaily.com, April 26, 2010. www.wnd.com.
Dan Stein	"What Arizona's Immigration Law Really Says," *Los Angeles Times*, April 30, 2010.
Jacob Sullum	"Arrest Everybody," *Reason*, March 4, 2010.
Robin Templeton	"Baby Baiting," *Nation*, July 29, 2010.
Julie M. Weise	"A Heavy Price to Ending Birthright Citizenship," *Los Angeles Times*, September 2, 2010.

OPPOSING
VIEWPOINTS®
SERIES

CHAPTER 3

What Is the Political Power of the U.S. Latino Community?

Chapter Preface

Every ten years, the United States Census Bureau conducts a national census that provides valuable information on the number and demographics of the people living in the country. Mandated by the US Constitution, the results of the census are used to allocate the number of seats in the US House of Representatives for each state, the number of electoral votes, and much-needed federal government funding. It also influences policy on education, health care, and crime prevention.

As the 2010 census was approaching, a controversy was brewing in the US Latino community. A number of Hispanic religious, political, and community leaders urged a nationwide boycott of the census by undocumented Hispanic workers. By not participating, they hoped to bring attention to the plight of undocumented workers and the need for immigration reform. As Miguel Rivera explains in an essay for CONLAMIC, an organization of Latino churches:

> April 1, 2010 marks Census Day—and for many undocumented Latino immigrants across America, the call to boycott the census is based on principle: immigration reform must be brought to policymakers' attention. It may be a radical approach—one especially difficult to understand or support for those unaffected by immigration policy—but the call serves an important purpose for undocumented and documented immigrants alike. The sadness and agony undocumented Latino individuals and their families endure is heartbreaking; it is my hope that through reform, their cause can be better understood and addressed.

Similar grass-roots campaigns to boycott the census sprang up in Arizona and New Mexico to protest state and local crackdowns on undocumented workers.

Rivera and other leaders of the boycott contended that for far too long, undocumented workers had been taken for granted—not just within the larger American community, but by Hispanic politicians and community activists, too. Hispanic workers are counted, thereby providing more political and economic clout to leaders in the community, but in return they get hassled by law enforcement, denied government services, and discriminated against by business and political interests. Moreover, in recent years they have become the targets of anti-immigration rhetoric and even hate crimes, boycott leaders claimed.

Critics of the boycott argued that such a move was counterproductive to helping the cause of immigration reform. An editorial published in *La Opinion*, the country's leading Spanish-language newspaper, called the boycott "a serious mistake" that "verges on political suicide." Arturo Vargas, the executive director of the National Association of Latino Elected Officials, maintained that the call for a boycott "may be well-intended but misguided and ultimately irresponsible." Hispanic political leaders and activists urged everyone to participate in the census, no matter their status, reminding them a boycott would send less money to states and cities that have large numbers of undocumented residents and could shift political clout elsewhere. In their opinion, the Hispanic community should be maximizing their political, economic, and social power, not undermining it.

The controversy over participation in the US Census is one of the subjects debated in the next chapter, which examines the political power of the US Latino community. Other viewpoints debate Latino electoral power and the need for Republicans and Democrats to attract Hispanic voters.

> *"Latinos formed their largest share ever of the national electorate [in 2008], 9 percent, and their numbers are poised to increase in every election to come."*

Latino Electoral Power Is Formidable

Alex Koppelman

Alex Koppelman is a staff writer for Salon, *an online magazine. In the following viewpoint, he reviews the numbers from the 2008 presidential election, noting that Latinos made a decisive difference in a number of states, including New Mexico, Florida, Colorado, and Nevada. Koppelman argues that both political parties are trying to appeal to the growing Latino demographics in these states.*

As you read, consider the following questions:

1. According to Koppelman, what is the Latino share of the national electorate?

2. In 2008, what was the share of the Latino electorate in New Mexico, as reported by the author?

Alex Koppelman, "A Permanent Democratic Majority," Salon.com, November 13, 2008. This article first appeared in Salon.com at http://www.salon.com. An online version remains in the *Salon* archives. Reprinted with permission.

3. How many Hispanics lived in the United States in 2008, according to Koppelman?

Over the past eight years, as much of the country went firmly into either the red [Republican] corner or the blue [Democrat] corner, New Mexico remained doggedly purple [a mixture of both Republican and Democrat]. In 2000, two of the state's three U.S. representatives were Republicans, as were its governor and one of its senators. But both houses of the state Legislature were run by Democrats, and Al Gore squeaked past George W. Bush [in the presidential race] in November, with a margin of fewer than 400 votes. Four years later, Democrat Bill Richardson won the governorship, but Bush captured New Mexico's five electoral votes, again by a small margin.

The Lessons of New Mexico

This year [2008] New Mexico didn't deliver any mixed messages. On Nov. 4, Democrats dominated at every level. Barack Obama beat John McCain, Tom Udall took an open Senate seat that had been Republican, and Martin Heinrich and Harry Teague took two formerly Republican House seats. And every one of them won in a landslide, with margins of 10 percent or more; Obama prevailed by 15 points, Udall by 22. New Mexico is now bright blue, with Democrats in nearly every elected statewide office, control of the state House and Senate, and an all Democratic congressional delegation.

What happened? The long-promised Latino realignment may have become reality. Coveted by [Bush administration adviser] Karl Rove, courted by George W. Bush, the fastest-growing sector of the American electorate stampeded toward the Democrats this November. New Mexico is only the most striking symbol of a nationwide trend that helped flip as many as seven states and 85 electoral votes into Obama's column. Latinos formed their largest share ever of the national electorate, 9 percent, and their numbers are poised to increase in every election to come. They also voted by their largest margin ever for the Democrats, 67 to 31 percent. If that pattern continues, the GOP [Republican Party] is doomed to 40 years of wandering in a desert.

In some of the purple and red states conquered by Obama, the degree to which Hispanic votes determined the outcome can be debated. Not in New Mexico. The bluing of New Mexico can be attributed almost solely to a change in the behavior of one demographic bloc. "If you look at the numbers, you'd have to say that it is because of the Latino vote," Cuauhtemoc "Temo" Figueroa, the Obama campaign's Latino vote director, says. "When you talk about New Mexico politics, it's not an afterthought, it's not an addendum, it *is* the discussion."

The Hispanic Demographic

In 2004, according to exit polls, Hispanics made up 32 percent of the electorate there, and broke 56-44 for John Kerry over Bush. But Bush, buoyed by the white vote, managed to win by 1 percentage point overall.

By 2008, the Hispanic share of the electorate had increased by a third, to 41 percent, and voters in the demographic were much more Democratic, going 69-30 for Obama over McCain. That change by itself can account for almost all of Obama's advantage in the state, especially since the white vote stayed essentially the same (though whites' share of the electorate was down by 7 percentage points) and the African-American population is small. This shift can also account for most of Udall's margin in his Senate race, and for the Democrats' wins in the two House races. It also means that the Hispanic share of the New Mexico electorate finally approaches the Hispanic share of the state population, which is 42 percent. (And this despite dire warnings from some quarters about widespread vote suppression in New Mexico.)

Top 10 Counties—Hispanic Population, 2008

		Hispanic Population
1	Los Angeles County, CA	4,702,785
2	Harris County, TX	1,564,845
3	Miami-Dade County, FL	1,496,595
4	Cook County, IL	1,229,964
5	Maricopa County, AZ	1,224,005
6	Orange County, CA	1,016,464
7	San Bernardino County, CA	957,866
8	Bexar County, TX	939,260
9	Dallas County, TX	938,672
10	San Diego County, CA	926,926

TAKEN FROM: Pew Hispanic Center and US Census Bureau data, 2008.

Experts who spoke to *Salon* also credited the Hispanic vote with delivering Colorado and Nevada to Obama. Colorado added a Democratic senator and a Democratic representative this cycle, while Nevada added a House seat. In both states, the Latino share of the electorate grew 50 percent or more from 2004 to 2008, from 10 percent to 15 percent in Nevada and from 8 to 13 percent in Colorado. Nevada's Hispanic margins for Obama were especially lopsided, at 76 to 24, according to exit polls.

Fernand Amandi, executive vice president of Bendixen & Associates, a firm known for its polling of Hispanics, says that even Obama's wins in Indiana, North Carolina and Virginia should be credited to this demographic cohort. Figueroa doesn't wholly disagree—he says that the Hispanic vote was "pivotal" in Indiana and "pivotal and determinative" in Virginia.

The Case of Florida

But the numbers were most striking in Florida, because of the history and unique nature of Florida's Latino electorate. For years, the state's Hispanic community was dominated by Cuban exiles, the devout Republicans crucial to the GOP's hold on the state's rich trove of electoral votes. This year, for the first time since such things began to be measured in the 1980s, Florida's Hispanics voted for a Democrat for president, and in large numbers too. In 2004, they went for Bush 56-44. This year, the result was almost the exact opposite; Obama took the community's vote, 57-42, and won the state.

Amandi says this change was the "largest swing of any demographic group in the country." He attributes it to the "rise of the non-Cuban Hispanic vote," an influx of people from other countries moving to Florida. (The Obama campaign made a special effort in the Orlando area, the center of the state's Puerto Rican community, a reliably Democratic bloc.) And as the exile generation ages and dies, the Cuban community is becoming less Republican too, Amandi says. Both trends bode poorly for the GOP's prospects in a swing state with 27 electoral votes.

None of this means that Democrats can take the Hispanic vote for granted. In fact, the party's success this year comes in large part because it began a concerted effort focusing on Hispanics. Simon Rosenberg, the president of the New Democrat Network, which has been studying the changing electorate and especially the impact of the Hispanic vote, says, "Increased turnout happened because Democrats finally woke up to this Hispanic opportunity ... It's really only in the last few years that Democrats woke up to this new reality. If you're a Hispanic voter, particularly in the Southwest or the West, the Democratic Party sort of woke up and started to speak to you."

Figueroa, too, credits the success to organization. "I think we've learned from previous elections and we've learned from

this election now that if you spend the resources and you pay attention to the community, you can win," he says. "The West in general is ripe territory for Democrats, and it's an area where you see not only the party structure investing huge amounts of resources in the West but progressive organizations investing a huge amount of time and money."

Looking to the Future

Assuming Democrats can keep up this momentum, a couple of big prizes await: Arizona and, yes, perhaps even Texas. The experts with whom *Salon* spoke were all but unanimous in saying that Arizona could be in play very soon, and that Texas could become a battleground within the next eight years and perhaps even by 2010.

"Whether in four years or whether in eight years, I do see potential there in Texas, because of just the sheer magnitude of the numbers, the Hispanic voters," Figueroa says. "But I think what has to happen in Texas is they—'they' meaning the party structure—have to show they can put together an operation that can win. And 2010 would be a great example to show where they're at."

If that happens, if Democrats can count on Hispanics to deliver the nine states, including those two, where their population is at or exceeds the national average, then the party would have a formidable advantage in every presidential election. Combined, those states represent 212 Electoral College votes. Add the dependably blue Northeast, and the Dems win the White House every time.

What the GOP Can Do

But just as Democrats can't take the Latino vote for granted, so can they not depend on the opposition to keep screwing up. For all the abuse heaped on him, Karl Rove saw the Hispanic juggernaut coming and tried to get the GOP ready. Rove had visions of appealing to Hispanics and thereby ensuring a political future for his party. And it almost worked, but then his fellow Republicans went nativist and mucked it all up.

"If the party doesn't embrace the kind of change that is out there in the way that our country's demographics are changing . . . they're going to relegate themselves to a perma- nent minority," says Dan Gurley, the Republican National Committee's field director during the 2004 election. "I think Karl Rove is absolutely right when it comes to where the party needs to be with the Hispanic community. I think he totally gets it, and the unfortunate thing is that a lot of people, a lot of the base of the party, don't."

There's an old political cliché: Demography is destiny. The Latino share of the national electorate has increased a full per- centage point in each of the last two national elections. It will only increase more quickly in the coming years, since so much of the Hispanic population, 46 million strong, consists of the U.S.-born children of nonvoting immigrants. The country's changing demographics left the GOP with a choice—prevent Hispanics from forming a reliably Democratic bloc or face what could be decades of minority party status. For the mo- ment, the Republican Party has chosen poorly. Now it's time to face the consequences.

> *"The Mexican-American vote is concen-
> trated in Democratic California and
> Republican Texas, so the Electoral Col-
> lege makes them less important in
> presidential elections than even their
> overall paltry numbers suggest."*

Latino Electoral Power Is Overrated

Steve Sailer

Steve Sailer is the film critic for the American Conservative *and
a columnist for VDARE.com. In the following viewpoint, he
maintains that the power of the Latino electorate does not live
up to the hype, as he finds that the Latino electorate has been
growing much less impressively than the Latino population as a
whole. Sailer argues that the black community still holds more
power in American culture and Latinos have yet to really exer-
cise their power at the ballot box, unlike other communities.*

As you read, consider the following questions:

1. According to projections by the Pew Research Center,
   cited by Sailer, how many Hispanics will there be in the
   United States in 2050?

Steve Sailer, "Is Brown the New Black?" *The American Conservative*, March 10, 2008. Reproduced by permission.

2. What percentage of the votes in the 2006 midterm elections were by Hispanic voters, according to the author?

3. According to a Pew-Kaiser poll, as cited by Sailer, what are the political views of the majority of Hispanic voters?

The slugfest between Barack Obama and Hillary Clinton [for the 2008 Democratic presidential nomination], in which only the most painstaking analyst can discern any disagreement over policy, highlights the ancient yet growing importance of ethnic identity in politics.

The race didn't start out that way. The 2007 polls showed that blacks favored Senator Clinton, the wife of "America's first black president," over Senator Obama, the preppie from paradise. Yet when the crunch came, four-fifths of black Democratic primary voters rallied to the yuppie technocrat's banner.

Shaken by the defection of an ethnicity Hillary had assumed was hereditarily hers, the Clinton campaign then pointed to the Latino vote as its "firewall." And in the important California primary, Hispanics did vote 67 percent to 32 percent for the former first lady. Elsewhere, however, the vaunted Hispanic bloc didn't quite live up to expectations. Hillary responded to her Super Tuesday woes by firing her Hispanic campaign manager, Patti Solis Doyle, and replacing her with Maggie Williams, who is black. As I write, Mrs. Clinton is left hoping that Latinos will bail her out in the upcoming Texas primary.

The Impact of Identity Politics

The multiracialization of American politics has barely begun. When it comes to identity politics, numbers count. And a new population projection from the Pew Research Center estimates that Hispanics will grow from 42 million in 2005 to a jaw-dropping 128 million in 2050. Meanwhile, African Americans will increase from 38 million to 57 million. (Caucasians will barely creep over the 200 million mark, presumably on the strength of Middle Eastern immigration.)

The relationship between blacks and Latinos will become increasingly central to American life, but it's a murky phenomenon, poorly understood by the white-dominated press.

Despite the hype, the Latino electorate has been growing much less impressively than the Latino population. Although Hispanics comprise about 15 percent of the residents of this country, they only cast 5.8 percent of the votes in the 2006 midterm elections, according to the Pew Hispanic Center's crunching of the raw data from the Census Bureau's big biennial voting survey. That was up from 5.3 percent in 2002—steady growth but hardly the political tsunami that we've been told about over and over. In contrast, blacks accounted for 10.3 percent of the vote, 77 percent more than Hispanics.

Thus it's far better, especially in the Democratic primaries, to get four-fifths of the black vote, as Obama does, than two-thirds of the Hispanic vote, as Mrs. Clinton does. Although Clinton has typically beaten Obama among whites, Obama does well enough that his large margin among black Democrats keeps him competitive (Clinton's secret weapon has been Asians, who sided with her 71-25 percent in California.)

The Black-Hispanic Relationship

One reason the black-Hispanic relationship is poorly understood is that class intersects with ethnicity in complex ways. At the bottom of society, among prison and street gangs, race rules. In the Los Angeles County jail, which is 60 percent Hispanic and 30 percent black, the two groups fought murderous battles in 2006. Last October, federal prosecutors accused the Florencia 13 street gang of trying to ethnically cleanse blacks from its unincorporated neighborhood in LA County. (The political impact of this violence shouldn't be exaggerated, though. The respectable folk who do most of the voting don't approve of gangbangers' feuding.)

In poorer neighborhoods, black residents feel uneasy about men speaking Spanish around them. Not being able to understand what is being said robs them of their street smarts. Are the two men next to you at the bus stop talking in Spanish about soccer or are they plotting to mug you? Who knows?

At the top of the power structure, in the House of Representatives and state legislatures, blacks and Latinos get along quite well, united by party (92 percent of elected Hispanics are Democrats) and a mutual desire to keep the affirmative action gravy train chugging along. Ward Connerly, a black opponent of ethnic quotas, has noted that when he was a regent of the University of California, the heaviest pressure on the regents to cheat on the anti-preference language written into the state constitution by Prop. 209 came not from the Black Caucus in the legislature but from the larger Latino Caucus. They threatened to cut UC's budget unless more Hispanic applicants were admitted.

Black politicians tend to view Hispanics today much as Irish politicos once saw their fellow Catholic Poles: silent partners in their coalition who should be grateful for their natural leaders' experience and charm. Not surprisingly, Hispanics don't agree. In some of the formerly all-black slum municipalities just south of Los Angeles, where Hispanics now make up the great majority of residents but only half of voters, ethnic politics has gotten nasty. But overall, Hispanic politicians know that time is on their side, so they can he patient about the arrogance of black colleagues.

In the middle levels of society, blacks and Latinos do compete. Relations aren't warm, but African-American men have tended to cede blue-collar jobs to immigrants without putting up massive resistance. Moreover, the swelling numbers and various dysfunctions of illegal immigrants generate numerous jobs for civil servants (who are typically required to be citizens). Therefore, many blacks are paid by taxpayers to teach, police, guard, administer, and otherwise deal with illegal aliens. It doesn't make for trans-ethnic amity, but it's a living.

America Ignores Latinos

There's another reason that black-Hispanic relations are poorly understood. Americans just don't pay much attention to Latinos. In American public discourse, Hispanics, especially Mexican-Americans, who now number about 30 million, remain what interstellar "dark matter" is to astrophysicists—a quantitatively significant yet mysteriously featureless aspect of the universe.

This is not for a lack of motivation on the part of America's corporate and political elites. Consultants have been trumpeting the growing numbers of Hispanics for a generation. Marketers have been lusting for the emergence of more Mexican-American celebrities to plug their products at least since Nancy Lopez's record-setting 1978 LPGA [Ladies' Professional Golf Association] rookie season made her the most popular female golfer ever.

Although the media constantly tries to drum up interest in Hispanics by extolling them as "swing voters" living in "vibrant neighborhoods" and so forth, the tedious reality is that the word that best sums up Latino America is inertia. Things just sort of keep on keeping on in the general direction that they were already moving. While Obama-mania sweeps the more fashion-frenzied white Democrats, Hispanics have stuck by the name brand they know.

Black Culture Still Dominates

Despite long-standing predictions that Americans will soon become fascinated by all things Latin, the public remains much more interested in African-Americans. In popular culture, trends flow from African-Americans to Mexican-Americans. The latter listen to hip-hop, but the former will not listen to music featuring accordions and trumpets. There have been exceptions—the bouncing lowrider cars that were popular in old-school rap videos were a Mexican-American invention—but black remains cooler than brown. Professional trendspotter Irma Zandl admitted in 2003 to *American Demographics,* a market research trade publication, that her biggest mistake had been predicting the increasing Latinization of American culture back in 1988. Fifteen years later, "there are still no mass fashion trends, no mass entertainment trends, no mass social trends rooted in the Hispanic culture." While there are a number of prominent Cubans, Puerto Ricans and other Caribbean Hispanics, there are still remarkably few famous Mexican-Americans.

Consider the forgotten man of the 2008 Democratic race, former energy secretary and UN ambassador Bill Richardson. Quantitatively, Richardson out-Obamas Obama. Is the Illinois senator half-minority? Well, the New Mexico governor is three-fourths minority. Did Obama live from ages 6 to 10 in a fairly important foreign country, Indonesia? Richardson lived from 1 to 13 among the power elite of the country that has the most direct impact on America, Mexico. But nobody cared, and Richardson quietly dropped out. Black simply trumps Mexican in the fascination sweepstakes.

This lack of interest hasn't stopped white commentators from theorizing about the impact of immigration they would find if they bothered to look. George Will, for instance, has long argued that Latin American immigration is solving America's racial problem, which he sees as resulting from the traditional American "one drop of blood" rule of thumb for determining race. South of the border, in contrast, racial lines are not as distinctly drawn.

Racial Politics

Yet after almost 500 years of intermarriage, most of Latin America still has a quite white ruling class. Darker men who rise up in society tend to marry fairer women, so their descendents are lighter-looking. Thus the genes of the successful rabble-rousers and self-made men get absorbed into the overclass.

It remains to be seen whether Hispanics turn the rest of America away from the one drop of blood theory or viceversa. Certainly, contra Will, Obama has only benefited from his ardent embrace of the one-drop rule. Although the candidate was raised by the white side of his family in multiracial Hawaii, where mixed-race children have been unexceptional for generations, he strenuously rejected Hawaiian haziness about racial identity. Obama moved to the black slums of Chicago to work as an ethnic activist, joined a stridently Afrocentrist church, and then went into discrimination law so he could sue white-run institutions. The lessons for ambitious young Hispanics would seem clear: ethnic solidarity among minorities is the American way to political success.

Latinos now have a full complement of civil-rights organizations, such as the National Council of La Raza (The Race), modeled on the black prototypes and usually well-subsidized by establishment heavyweights such as the Ford Foundation. Still, copying the black grievance machine hasn't quite paid off as well as Latino activists had hoped. The institutions are staffed by would-be Alberto Sharptons and Jesus Jacksons, but these leaders tend to lack followers. For example, Hispanic politicians' protests over Clinton firing Solis Doyle barely made a ripple. One impediment is a low level of trust of strangers, including co-ethnics, among Latinos. Harsh experience has taught Mexicans to put little faith in anybody beyond the extended family.

When millions of illegal immigrants waving Mexican flags and demanding amnesty marched in the streets of America in the spring of 2006, the English-language media was baffled as to which shadowy leaders had turned these throngs out. (The chief answer proved unexciting: funny disc jockeys on Spanish-language radio stations.) And when the illegal aliens didn't show up at the 2007 marches, the English-language media didn't know why either.

The language barrier is one clear reason for the charisma gap between African-Americans and Latinos. Yet the Manhattan-Beltway center-right pundits' assumption that Hispanics are all new immigrants who will assimilate seamlessly as soon as they learn English is wrong. For example, Sen. Ken Salazar claims his ancestors arrived in Santa Fe before the Mayflower landed at Plymouth Rock. Hispanics have a long history in America, yet other Americans haven't much noticed, which allows white intellectuals to make up whatever theories they prefer *a priori* [as a given] about what Hispanic immigration portends.

In contrast, African-American history does not lack publicity. A new study by a Stanford researcher asked 2,000 high-school juniors and seniors to name the ten most famous Americans who weren't presidents. The top three were Martin Luther King Jr., Rosa Parks, and Harriet Tubman. Although Hispanics now make up over one-fifth of public school students, there were no Spanish surnames on this top-ten list.

Disappointing Impact at the Ballot Box

Neither do they make much impact at the ballot box. Many are illegal aliens. Moreover, legal immigrants from Mexico are less likely than any other nationality to bother becoming U.S. citizens. (Although American whites tend to see Mexico as tragic and comic, Mexican immigrants love their native land and dream of returning home for their retirement.) And Mexican-American citizens are less likely to register and vote. They tend to find the drama of their private lives more compelling than public affairs.

Hispanics do find their way to the polls in the presidential elections at slightly higher percentages than in the more boring midterm races—6.0 percent in 2004, up from 5.4 percent in 2000. Still, it's unlikely they will reach 7.0 percent of voters in 2008. Plus, the Mexican-American vote is concentrated in Democratic California and Republican Texas, so the Electoral College makes them less important in presidential elections than even their overall paltry numbers suggest.

Nor are illegal aliens a hot-button issue for Latinos, as Obama discovered to his pain in California where he campaigned in favor of issuing drivers licenses to illegal aliens, while Hillary was on record as being opposed. A 2002 Pew-Kaiser poll of 2,929 registered Hispanic voters found 48 percent believe there are too many immigrants in this country, while only 7 percent said there are too few.

But when the pollsters rephrased the question to specifically mention "Latin American immigrants," the Hispanic voters switched, with 36 percent now saying "Allow more" and only 21 percent choosing "Reduce the number." Evidently, while immigration can be exploited as an emotional ethnic pride issue among Hispanic voters, on objective grounds most Latino voters are negative toward illegal aliens. After all, they bear the brunt of the lower wages, overcrowded housing, and overwhelmed public schools and hospitals. However, their ambivalence toward illegal immigration is not reflected among their self-appointed leaders, whose interest lies in simply boosting the number of warm brown bodies they can claim to represent.

Politics of Hispanic Electorate

In general, Hispanic voters tend to be old-fashioned tax-and-spend Democrats. In the Pew-Kaiser poll, 60 percent of Hispanics said they "would prefer to pay higher taxes to support a larger government that provides more services" compared to 35 percent of whites. Tax-and-spend politics reflect self-interest on the part of Hispanics since they tend to cluster below the national average in income and education. And they do not get much more conservative as they go up the income ladder, perhaps because higher education means more exposure to the multiculturalist mindset reigning on college campuses.

Mexican immigrants don't bring much human capital with them. The Census Bureau recently estimated that while more than 40 percent of recent immigrants from India have an advanced degree, only about 1 percent of Mexican immigrants do. In fact, over 60 percent of Mexican immigrants have less than a high school diploma. While about 20 percent of African immigrants work in "science, engineering, technology, or health," only about 1 percent of Mexicans do. Those who have what it takes to make it big in Mexico stay home. That may help explain why there are so few high-profile Mexican-Americans.

The Assimilation Question

Pundits frequently claim that Hispanics either will or will not "assimilate," although this always begs the question "assimilate toward whom?" It's hard for many white intellectuals to remember that there are people in this world whose highest aspiration is *not* to Be Like Me.

Some Latino youths, for instance, are attracted by the glamour of African-American norms. For example, the Hispanic illegitimacy rate has grown from 19 percent in 1980 to 50 percent in 2006 (compared to 71 percent for blacks and 27 percent for whites).

That middle position is characteristic. In recent decades, Latinos have generally fallen midway between whites and blacks on most social statistics. For instance, the Hispanic imprisonment rate is 2.9 times the white imprisonment rate, while the black rate is 7.2 times more. (In contrast, the Asian imprisonment rate is only 0.22 as high.)

Latin American immigrant families tend to make strong educational progress from the first generation to the second. After that, things slow down. In 1992, the last time the National Assessment of Educational Progress test asked if students were born in the U.S., the school achievement test gap between whites and American-born Hispanics was two-thirds as large as the notoriously deleterious one between the whites and blacks.

In addition, some behavior gets worse as immigrants assimilate—illegitimacy goes up and the crime rate appears to be significantly higher among American-born Hispanics. In reality, assimilation isn't a black or white question but a statistical one. We can be sure that some Hispanics will assimilate toward middle-class white lives, some toward underclass black customs, and many will continue to follow working-class Hispanic traditions.

The Case of New Mexico

Consider New Mexico, which has been home to Hispanics for four centuries and is now 44 percent Latino. Although it's on the border, it doesn't attract as many immigrants as Arizona, so its assimilated Hispanics should be doing well, right? In 2007, Tim Russert humiliated New Mexico Gov. Bill Richardson on "Meet the Press" by reading off New Mexico's ranking among the 50 states on a scale where one is best:

> Percent of people living below the poverty line, you're 48. Percent of children below, 48. Median family income, 47. People without health insurance, 49. Children without health insurance, 46. Teen high school dropouts, 47. Death rate due to firearms, 48. Violent crime rate, 46.

Of course, it's hardly Richardson's fault that in five years as governor, he hadn't succeeded in turning New Mexicans into Minnesotans.

The sheer size of the upcoming Hispanic population makes the statistics ominous. Assume that Hispanic individuals are only, say, one-third as likely as African-Americans to fall into the underclass. That's not so bad, right? Yet in 40 years, there will be three times as many Hispanics as there are blacks today, so the Latino underclass would then be as big as the black underclass is today.

Interesting Times

It would be imprudent to assume that Hispanics in America will forever remain politically quiescent under uncharismatic leaders. There is tremendous pressure from within America on Hispanics to follow the path of blacks in politicizing their grievances and developing a culture of rejection. A young high-school history teacher in Arizona told me that he had initially been disturbed when his Latino students accused him of racism: "Why can't I turn in my homework late? You let Julio turn his in late. That's racist!" He finally realized, though, that "racist" was simply the word they had been taught by American culture to mean "unfair."

Nor is Latin American history uniformly dull. It's actually quite unpredictable. For example, after more than three decades of stable, unchallenged rule, the Mexican dictator Porfirio Díaz was suddenly overthrown in 1911. The Mexican Revolution went on to kill perhaps one million people. As he fled to exile in Paris, Díaz is said to have reflected, like a proto-Yogi Berra, "In Mexico, nothing ever happens until it happens."

Similarly, much of Latin America is currently excited over the rise of leftist populist *presidentes* preaching racial resentment, such as Hugo Chavez in Venezuela and Evo Morales in Bolivia.

Whether this "wind from the south" will ever reach America is impossible to foresee, but we may eventually be living in interesting times.

"Democratic candidates are vying to attract Latinos like never before."

Democrats Are Courting Latino Voters

Jennifer Parker

Jennifer Parker is a reporter for ABC News. In the following viewpoint, she reviews the efforts of 2008 Democratic presidential candidates to woo Latino voters, a demographic she identifies as vital for future electoral success. Parker also reports that many Hispanic leaders call the immigration strategy of the Republican Party (GOP) a political disaster that will drive more Latinos to vote for Democratic candidates and mobilize against anti-immigrant GOP policies.

As you read, consider the following questions:

1. What minority group represented nearly half the total US population growth between 2002 and 2006, according to the Pew Hispanic Center, as cited by Parker?

2. As reported by the author, what minority group represented about 10 percent of the US electorate in 2008?

3. According to a June 2007 poll cited by Parker, do more Hispanics identify as Democrats or Republicans?

Jennifer Parker, "Democratic Candidates Court Latino Voters," ABCNews.com, September 7, 2007. Reproduced by permission.

As part of an effort to woo the nation's rapidly growing Hispanic population, all but one of the Democratic presidential candidates converge at a first-of-its-kind debate at the University of Miami Sunday [September 9, 2007].

The 90-minute forum will be televised nationally in prime time on Univision, the most watched Spanish-language television network in the United States.

"For the first time in U.S. history, a debate will focus exclusively on Latino issues," said Simon Rosenberg, president of the centrist New Democratic Network, a political advocacy organization.

However, New Mexico Gov. Bill Richardson, the only Hispanic presidential candidate, has been asked to refrain from showing off his fluent Spanish-speaking skills. Questions will be asked and answered in English, and then translated into Spanish for the network's TV, radio and online platforms.

All of the Democratic presidential candidates agreed to the debate. However Sen. Joe Biden, D-Del., pulled out on Friday.

His office said he will be too busy after just getting back from a trip to Iraq, appearing on a Sunday morning talk show on Sunday, and preparing for Tuesday's Senate hearing assessing Iraq's stability.

A similar Hispanic debate for the Republican presidential candidates scheduled for Sept. 16 [2007] was canceled because Sen. John McCain, R-Ariz., was the only candidate who said he could attend. McCain supported the failed immigration reform effort in the Senate.

Hispanic Voters a 'Battleground Community'

Latinos are the nation's largest minority group, representing nearly half the total population growth between 2002 and 2006, according to the Pew Hispanic Center. Hispanics will represent about 10 percent of the U.S. electorate in 2008.

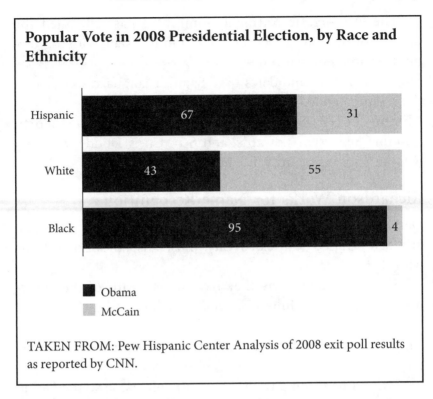

Popular Vote in 2008 Presidential Election, by Race and Ethnicity

TAKEN FROM: Pew Hispanic Center Analysis of 2008 exit poll results as reported by CNN.

In a close contest, analysts say Hispanics could make the difference in who finishes first—providing they come out to vote.

Political strategists say the debate is a key part of a tactical strategy to win the support of Latino voters in key battleground states such as Nevada, Colorado, New Mexico, Arizona and Florida, where the Hispanic population is rising.

"This is a battleground community of huge consequence that could decide the next president of the United States," Rosenberg said.

Democratic Candidates Court Latino Voters

With immigration reform emerging as a top issue in 2008, Democratic candidates are vying to attract Latinos like never before.

The Democratic National Committee has scheduled the party's convention in Denver; Colorado is a state with a growing Hispanic population.

Many of the candidates have Spanish-language sections on their campaign Web sites, including Richardson, Sen. Hillary Clinton, D-NY., Sen. Barack Obama, D-Ill., former North Carolina Sen. John Edwards, and Sen. Chris Dodd, D-Conn., who also speaks Spanish fluently.

Richardson Works for Name Recognition

Despite having a mother who is Mexican, being fully bilingual and being raised in Mexico City, most Hispanics don't know who Richardson is.

Six in 10 Latinos say they have never heard of the governor, according to a June *USA Today*/Gallup study.

"With a name like Bill Richardson, it's a bit of a challenge," said Tom Reynolds, Richardson's national press secretary.

"His name is not a traditional Hispanic name so the Latino community doesn't readily make that connection." he said.

The Richardson campaign recently launched "Mi Familia"—a grassroots fundraising and support-building effort directed toward Hispanics in Arizona, Nevada and California.

"Latinos won't vote for us just because the governor is Latino," Reynolds said. "He is equally concerned as they are about health care, Iraq, education and energy, so our message is just as important as our shared heritage."

Clinton Won Democratic Latino Voters

Clinton may have an edge with the Hispanic community. Her husband garnered 72 percent of support of Latino voters in 1996, according to exit polls.

She has also highlighted her close relationships with prominent Hispanics, including her campaign manager, Patricia Solis Doyle, the first Latino woman to lead a presidential campaign, Sen. Bob Menendez, D-N.J., and Dolores Huerta, a longtime activist who helped Cesar Chavez organize farmworkers.

She has hired a Hispanic pollster and a director of Hispanic outreach, and has some high-profile endorsements, including Fabian Núñez, speaker of the California House, and Los Angeles Mayor Antonio Villaraigosa.

"The relationship that she started with the Latino community didn't start yesterday," said Fabiola Rodríguez-Ciampoli, director of Hispanic outreach for the Clinton campaign.

A June [2007] USA Today/Gallup Poll found that Hispanics, by nearly 3 to 1, say they're Democrats or lean that way. Of those, 59 percent said they support Clinton, while only 13 percent said they support Obama. That support could translate into a huge political asset in early contests in Florida, California, Nevada and other states with large Hispanic populations.

"People know she has a strong record of supporting issues important to our community like heath care, education, Iraq and immigration," Rodríguez-Ciampoli said.

Clinton and Obama spoke before roughly 2,000 Hispanic educators, activists, and community and business leaders at the annual conference of the nation's largest Hispanic civil rights organization, the National Council of La Raza, in Miami Beach in July.

Obama Emphasizes Joint Struggles

At the forum, Clinton touted her personal connection to the community while Obama emphasized the intertwined struggles of black and Hispanic Americans. Both support a path to legalization for illegal immigrants, improved border security and universal health care and preschool.

For his part, Obama has run Spanish-language radio ads in Nevada. He has an independent Web site devoted to his campaign—amigosdeobama.com—complete with a Latin-flavored theme song.

And he has a full-time staffer in charge of Hispanic outreach efforts.

Obama voted "yes" on legislation that includes a fence along the U.S.-Mexico border and is in favor of increased security, but like Clinton, has advocated finding a legal path to allow 12 million illegal immigrants to earn citizenship and remain in the United States.

Edwards, another leading Democratic president candidate, has barely registered on Latinos' charts.

Republicans Made Inroads

The vast majority of Latino voters usually vote Democratic. However the GOP [Republican Party] made significant gains in attracting Hispanic voters in the 2000 and 2004 elections.

President [George W.] Bush drew Latino voters to the GOP like no Republican before him. His campaign outspent former Vice President Al Gore in 2000 in the crucial state of Florida, where a majority of Cuban-Americans reside.

In 2004, Bush won 40 percent of the Latino vote, doubling the number of Hispanics who had supported Republican Bob Dole eight years earlier.

But the inroads Bush made are vanishing and may be gone by the time November 2008 rolls around.

GOP Immigration Strategy

The Latino community was mobilized to the streets to protest a House bill calling for the criminalization of all undocumented workers—a bill passed in the GOP-led House but not passed in the Senate.

Proposals for more walls and fences along the U.S.-Mexico border and the failure of Congress to pass immigrant legislation may mobilize Hispanics further.

"The GOP's anti-immigration strategy has been a political disaster for the Republicans," Rosenberg said, pointing to ads the Republican Party ran in 25 states before the 2006 midterm elections that equated Mexican immigrants with Islamic terrorists.

While turnout increased among Latino voters in 2006, support for Republican candidates decreased to 30 percent.

Joe Garcia, director of the Hispanic Strategy Center at the National Democratic Network, predicts Hispanics will turn away from Republicans at the polls in 2008 because of the anti-immigration policies of Republican presidential candidates Rep. Tom Tancredo, R-Colo., and Rep. Duncan Hunter, R-Ariz.

"The field of candidates has been pulled to the right by these xenophobes and racists," he said. "There is not an Hispanic in America who doesn't know who Tom Tancredo is and that's going to have an effect."

| "*Republicans have got to make headway with [the Latino] population.*"

Republicans Must Court Latino Voters

Star Parker

Star Parker is a syndicated columnist, a political commentator, and the founder of CURE, a think tank. In the following viewpoint, she acknowledges that the Republican Party needs to attract the growing Latino community by reminding them that it is within their best interests to support Republican policies.

As you read, consider the following questions:

1. According to Census data cited by Parker, what percentage of children born in the United States between July 2008 and July 2009 were "nonwhite minorities"?

2. What demographic group accounts for almost 55 percent of the US population growth, according to the author?

3. What state was designated to be the worst state in the country for doing business by *Chief Executive* magazine, as reported by Parker?

Star Parker, "Can the Republicans Win the Hispanic Vote," CURE.org, June, 14, 2010. Reproduced by permission of the author.

New Census data show the continued trend that the United States is becoming a nation increasingly less white. According to this latest report, 48.6 percent of children born in the U.S. between July 2008 and July 2009 were "nonwhite minorities." That's up 2 percentage points from two years earlier, and soon the figure will cross the 50 percent mark. The largest growth demographic is Hispanics, who accounted for almost 55 percent of our population growth. And, most of this growth—two-thirds—came from births, not from immigration.

Changing Demographics

Aside from the knowledge that the country is becoming more colorful, an obvious thing we've got to be thinking about is what this means politically. Given that Democrats have been getting the majority of Hispanic and black votes—the two largest minorities—the straightforward conclusion appears to be that demographic trends favor the Democratic Party.

In the 2008 elections, white voters, for the first time ever, accounted for less than 75 percent of the total vote. It's been noted that if each ethnic group voted as it did in 2008, but made up the same percentage of the electorate as it did 20 years ago, John McCain would be our president today.

Clearly, demographic realities present real challenges to the Republican Party and the values that it is supposed to be championing—limited government and free markets.

Most recent polling from Gallup shows Hispanics generically favoring Democrats over Republicans by 2 to 1.

Republicans have got to make headway with this population.

Republicans Have Work to Do

We need them for building the political consensus to make the critical changes to fix our country—cutting the massive growth in government Democrats have put in motion, cutting

"So the republicans are targeting Hispanic voters? . . ." Cartoon by Baloo (Rex May). www.CartoonStock.com.

spending to eliminate trillion-dollar deficits, reducing our now massive $13 trillion debt and coming up with creative solutions to the $100 trillion in unfunded liabilities we're now looking at in our major entitlement programs—Social Security and Medicare. And, of course, holding the line on taxes.

Otherwise stated, if Republicans cannot start pulling in a bigger chunk of this Hispanic vote, it will be tough to be optimistic that we'll be able to reverse the direction Democrats have initiated—transformation of our country into a European-style social-welfare state.

Can Republicans reverse this political trend?

I say yes. The reason is that it is in the interests of our Hispanic citizens to support what Republicans are trying to do.

We've got in front of us right now two contrasting snapshots of what America's future could look like. These two snapshots happen to be our two states with the nation's largest Hispanic populations. California and Texas.

The Case of California

California today is America's Greece [a nation in dire economic straits]. Overgoverned, overtaxed, overregulated, overunionized, with excessive spending and impossible entitlements commitments. If you want to know the path our federal government is now on, just look at California.

In a recent survey by *Chief Executive* magazine, CEOs rated California as the worst state in the country for doing business. It is the only state they awarded a grade of "F" in the category of "Taxation and Regulation."

Over the last year and a half, California lost over a million jobs, and its overall level of employment is down from where it was 10 years ago. Its unemployment rate is several points above the national average.

The Texas Model

Texas, on the other hand, was rated No. 1 by CEOs. In a low-tax, low-regulation, right-to-work state, unemployment in Texas is several points below the national average. And Texas has had net positive job creation through the recent recession.

Hispanics who think California is a model for America's future can keep voting for Democrats. But my guess is most will prefer the Texas model.

If Republicans make this choice clear to these folks, political change has got to happen.

Periodical and Internet Sources Bibliography

The following articles have been selected to supplement the diverse views presented in this chapter.

Mona Charen	"Republicans Shouldn't Alienate Hispanic Voters," *National Review*, May 4, 2010.
Elise Foley	"The DREAM ACT and Latino Voters," *Washington Independent*, September 22, 2010.
Jack Kerwick	"Arizona, Minorities, and Republicans," *Intellectual Conservative*, May 12, 2010.
Steve Kornacki	"Has Immigration Really Been the GOP's Problem?" *Salon*, July 7, 2010. www.salon.com.
Nikolas Kozloff	"Obama's Electoral Dilemma," *Counterpunch*, June 5, 2008.
Steve Malanga	"The Latino Voting Trickle," *City Journal*, Winter 2009.
Joe Pace	"When the Right Filibusters Its Own Ideals to Death," *Salon*, September 22, 2010. www.salon.com.
Amanda Paulson	"DREAM Act: Is Harry Reid Angling for Hispanic Votes?" *Christian Science Monitor*, September 21, 2010.
Tom Tancredo	"The Truth About Republicans and the 'Hispanic Vote,'" WorldNetDaily.com, March 20, 2010. www.wnd.com.
Luisita Lopez Torregrosa	"Democrats Court Hispanics with Promises, Pleas, and the DREAM Act," Politics Daily, September 20, 2010. www.politicsdaily.com.

OPPOSING
VIEWPOINTS®
SERIES

CHAPTER 4

What Social Issues Impact the U.S. Latino Community?

Chapter Preface

The debate over health-care reform has raged for years in the United States. Leaders of both major political parties have been concerned over rising health-care costs: the United States has the highest health-care costs in the world relative to the size of its economy. Another troubling statistic for politicians, activists, and health-care officials is that approximately 30 million Americans do not have health insurance coverage. Many economists began to emphasize that getting health-care costs under control was integral to the long-term fiscal viability of the US economy.

With the election of Barack Obama in 2008, health-care reform became one of the administration's first priorities. One of his campaign promises was to pass reform that would increase coverage and decrease costs. After a rancorous period of debate, the Congress passed two bills: the Patient Protection and Affordable Care Act, which was passed as law on March 23, 2010, and an amended bill, the Health Care and Education Reconciliation Act of 2010, which became law on March 30, 2010.

The debate surrounding the bill was distinctive for its venom and passion. Opponents of health-care reform enumerated several problems with the proposed reforms: worries about increased taxes, more government spending, mandates on insurance coverage, less choice on doctors and procedures, and whether the government would be subsidizing abortions.

Those opposed to the proposed reforms were also concerned that undocumented workers would be eligible for benefits under the new law. Many of the people opposed to health-care reform were also the same people against immigration reform. They were adamantly opposed to undocumented workers coming across the border and draining the US health system and demanded that any reform directly and strictly prohibit undocumented workers from being able to benefit from it.

The sometimes strong rhetoric from opponents of health-care reform led many who supported it to charge opponents with thinly veiled racism. They traced history, noting that earlier attempts to create a universal welfare state in the United States have been overwhelmed by accusations of "welfare queens" or drug dealers trying to game the system and rip off US taxpayers. They maintain that the hostility to a universal welfare state in some quarters is directly connected to an unwillingness to subsidize programs that would benefit minorities.

Health-care reform opponents denied any charges of racist resentment, arguing that they were being painted with a wide brush. Just because one is opposed to health-care reform does not mean one is a racist, they contended. Moreover, they argued, because a few opponents have used racist rhetoric to deride health-care reform, that should not tar the entire anti-health-care reform movement.

The issue of whether racial resentment played a role in the health-care debate is one of the topics examined in the next chapter, which takes a look at some of the social issues that impact the US Latino community. Other topics include the efficacy of bilingual education and the impact of Hispanic economic power.

> "In a country as diverse as the United States, fluency in the common tongue is an essential bond among citizens, and the experience of learning it alongside classmates of different ethnic origins reinforces the message that Americans share a common culture."

Bilingual Education Is a Barrier to Hispanic Assimilation

Heather Mac Donald

Heather Mac Donald is a fellow at the Manhattan Institute and contributing editor at the institute's City Journal. *In the following viewpoint, she maintains that bilingual education should be banned. Mac Donald points out the success of the 1998 California ban that has resulted in higher test scores among Hispanic students.*

As you read, consider the following questions:

1. How did Manuel Ramirez II describe the aim of bilingual education, according to Mac Donald?

Heather Mac Donald, "The Bilingual Ban That Worked," *City Journal*, Autumn 2009. Reproduced by permission.

2. What does the author point to as a patent inequity in the bilingual education crusade?

3. What example does Mac Donald provide to prove the success of immersion education?

In 1998, Californians voted to pass Proposition 227, the "English for the Children Act," and dismantle the state's bilingual-education industry. The results, according to California's education establishment, were not supposed to look like this: button-cute Hispanic pupils at a Santa Ana elementary school boasting about their English skills to a visitor. Those same pupils cheerfully calling out to their principal on their way to lunch: "Hi, Miss Champion!" A statewide increase in English proficiency among all Hispanic students.

Instead, warned legions of educrats, eliminating bilingual education in California would demoralize Hispanic students and widen the achievement gap. Unless Hispanic children were taught in Spanish, the bilingual advocates moaned, they would be unable to learn English or to succeed in other academic subjects.

California's electorate has been proved right: Hispanic test scores on a range of subjects have risen since Prop. 227 became law. But while the curtailment of California's bilingual-education industry has removed a significant barrier to Hispanic assimilation, the persistence of a Hispanic academic underclass suggests the need for further reform.

Bilingual Education's Political Agenda

The counterintuitive linguistic claims behind bilingual education were always a fig leaf covering a political agenda. The 1960s Chicano rights movement ("Chicano" refers to Mexican-Americans) asserted that the American tradition of assimilation was destroying not just Mexican-American identity but also Mexican-American students' capacity to learn. Teaching these students in English rather than in Spanish hurt their self-esteem and pride in their culture, Chicano activists alleged: hence the high drop-out rates, poor academic performance, and gang involvement that characterized so many Mexican-American students in the Southwest. Manuel Ramirez III, currently a psychology professor at the University of Texas at Austin, argued that bilingual education was necessary to ensure "the academic survival of Chicano children and the political and economic strength of the Chicano community." The role of American schools, according to this nascent ideology, became the preservation of the Spanish language and Mexican culture for Mexican-origin U.S. residents.

Novel linguistic theories arose to buttress this political platform. Children could not learn a second language well unless they were already fully literate in their native tongue, the newly minted bilingual-ed proponents argued. To teach English to a five-year-old who spoke Spanish at home, you had to instruct him in Spanish for several more years, until he had mastered Spanish grammar and spelling. "Young children are not language sponges," asserts McGill University psychology professor Fred Genesee, defying centuries of parental observation. Even more surprisingly, the advocates suddenly discovered that the ability to learn a second language improved with age—news to every adult who has struggled through do-it-yourself language recordings.

Such ad hoc justifications rested on shaky scientific ground. Psycholinguistics research supports what generations of immigrants experienced firsthand: the younger you are when you tackle a second language, the greater your chances of achieving full proficiency. Children who learn a second language early in life may even process it in the same parts of the brain that process their first language, an advantage lost as they age.

Only one justification for bilingual education made possible sense. The bilingual theorists maintained that children should be taught academic content—physics, say, or history—in their home language, lest they fall behind their peers in their knowledge of subject matter. But this argument applied most forcefully where bilingual education has always been the rarest: in high school, where, one would hope, teachers use relatively sophisticated concepts. In the earliest grades, however, where bilingual education has always been concentrated, academic content is predominantly learning a language—how to read and write B-A-T, for example. Moreover, most Hispanic children who show up in American elementary school have subpar Spanish skills to begin with, so teaching them in Spanish does not provide a large advantage over English in conveying knowledge about language—or anything else.

Patent Inequities

The bilingual-education crusade also contained patent inequities that never seemed to trouble its advocates. If teaching a nonnative speaker in his home tongue was such a boon—if it was, as many argued, a civil right—bilingual education should have been provided to every minority-language group, not just to Hispanics, who have been almost the exclusive beneficiaries of the practice. If instructing non-English-speaking students in English was destructive, it would damage a school's sole Pashto speaker just as much as its Hispanic majority. But minority rights, usually the proud battle cry of self-styled progressives, invariably crumpled before brute political power when it came to bilingual ed. "If it could benefit 82 percent of the kids, you don't have to offer it to everyone," says Robert Linquanti, a project director for the government-supported research organization WestEd.

Nor did bilingual-education proponents pause long before counterevidence. In 1965, just as the movement was getting under way in the United States, the Canadian province of Quebec decided that not enough Quebecois children were learning French. It instituted the most efficient method for overcoming that deficit: immersion. Young English-speaking students started spending their school days in all-French classes, emerging into English teaching only after having absorbed French. By all accounts, the immersion schools have been successful. And no wonder: the simple insight of immersion is that the more one practices a new language, the better one learns it. Students at America's most prestigious language academy, the Middlebury Language Schools, pledge not to speak a word of English once the program begins, even if they are beginners in their target languages. "If you go back to speaking English, the English patterns will reassert themselves and interfere with acquisition of the new grammatical patterns," explains Middlebury vice president Michael Geisler.

Language Immersion Theory

McGill professor Genesee—who opposed Prop. 227 in 1998, when he was directing the education school at the University of California at Davis—hates it when proponents of English immersion in America point to the success of French immersion in Quebec. The English-speaking Quebecois don't risk losing English, Genesee says, since it remains the predominant Canadian tongue and is a "high-prestige language."

Whereas if you start American Hispanics off in English, Genesee maintains, "they won't want to speak Spanish" because it is a "stigmatized, low-prestige language." Genesee's argument exposes the enduring influence of Chicano political activism on academic bilingual theory. Hispanic students do risk losing their home tongue when taught in the majority language. Such linguistic oblivion has beset second- and third-generation immigrants throughout American history—not because of the relative status of their home languages but simply because of the power of language immersion and the magnetic force of the public culture. But bilingual-ed proponents know that most Americans don't view preserving immigrants' home tongues as a school responsibility. So they publicly promote bilingual education as a pedagogically superior way to teach Hispanics English and other academic subjects, even as they privately embrace the practice as a means for ensuring that Hispanic students preserve their Spanish.

The early Chicano activists sought the "replacement of assimilationist ideals ... with cultural pluralism," writes University of Houston history professor Guadalupe San Miguel, Jr. in his book *Contested Policy*. Bilingual education was the activists' primary weapon in fighting assimilation because, as they rightly understood, English-language teaching is a powerful tool for encouraging assimilation. In a country as diverse as the United States, fluency in the common tongue is an essential bond among citizens, and the experience of learning it alongside classmates of different ethnic origins reinforces the message that Americans share a common culture. Bilingual-ed proponents often accuse immersion advocates of opposing multilingualism or wanting to stamp out Spanish. This is nonsense. But it is true that maintaining students' home language for the sake of strengthened ethnic identity is no part of a school's mandate. Its primary language duty, rather, is to ensure that citizens can understand one another and participate in democracy.

> *"No recent research comparing English-only versus bilingual [education] models has found English-only approaches to be more effective at teaching English. In fact, most program model comparisons have shown bilingual models to be more effective."*

Bilingual Education Is the Best Approach for English Language Learners

Jeff Bale

Jeff Bale teaches language and language education in the Department of Teacher Education at Michigan State University. In the following viewpoint, he finds that opposition to bilingual education is often based on myths and political arguments against non-English speakers. The evidence shows, Bale argues, that bilingual education is very effective for teaching English to non-English speakers.

Jeff Bale, "The Fight for Bilingual Education," *International Socialist Review*, January-February 2010. Reproduced by permission.

As you read, consider the following questions:

1. In the 2004–2005 school year, how many emergent bilinguals, or students learning English, does Bale say there were in America?

2. What five states have the highest percentage of emergent bilinguals, according to the author?

3. According to a recent American Federation of Teachers report cited by Bale, what percent of emergent bilinguals are educated in English-only programs?

One of the most urgent—and misunderstood—issues facing U.S. public education today is meeting the needs of students who are not yet proficient in the English language. . . . *The Invisible Minority*, a 1966 report by the National Education Association task force on education in the Southwest [is significant]. This study intersected with the struggle for Chicano civil rights that would lead to the passage of the Bilingual Education Act (BEA) of 1968. The BEA represented one of the most significant advances in the education of "emergent bilingual" [also called English language learners] students in two ways. It consolidated the gains in bilingual and bicultural programs that were fought for, often school-by-school, in the Southwest and West. Additionally, as part of official federal educational policy, the BEA legitimized what educators and activists had known for some time, namely that students learning English had specific educational rights, including the right to be educated in their home language.

Hardly had the ink dried on the BEA, however, when attacks on the legitimacy of bilingual education began. . . . The clock has been turned back on the gains made in bilingual-bicultural education in the late sixties and early seventies.

To be sure, plenty of educational and linguistic research has deepened our understanding of how children learn languages and which classroom practices aid that process. Likewise, much is known about which educational policies support language learning and which policies thwart it. However, the education of emergent bilingual students remains misunderstood in large part because so little attention is paid to how past movements against racism and for immigrant rights have improved the education of all children, but especially of emergent bilingual students. This article reviews the history of this connection. My main argument is that advances (and setbacks) in antiracist and pro-immigrant struggles have had the most significant impact on the academic and linguistic welfare of emergent bilingual students in public schools. While this argument may seem self-evident, the reality today is that those most dedicated to improving the education of emergent bilinguals too often miss the forest for the trees: while effective classroom practices and sympathetic policies matter, they wilt in the face of segregation, racism, and attacks on immigrant rights. . . .

Emergent Bilinguals and Their Educational Experiences Today

While language diversity has always been a feature of public schools in this country, the population of emergent bilinguals has changed dramatically in the last two decades. The most recent analysis of enrollments from pre-school through grade twelve (P–12) reported that in the 2004–05 school year, approximately 5.12 million students were emergent bilinguals, about 10.5 percent of the total P–12 population. Moreover, the emergent bilingual population has increased by over 110 percent in the last fifteen years—seven times more rapidly than general P–12 enrollments. These averages, of course, mask huge disparities in distribution. Just five states—California, Texas, New York, Florida, and Illinois—were home to 68 percent of all emergent bilinguals, according to the 2000 Census. Second, the rate of growth between 1990 and 2000 exceeded 200 percent in six states: Nevada, Nebraska, South Dakota, Georgia, Arkansas, and Oregon. This remarkable growth is not simply tied to immigration: the majority of emergent bilinguals at both primary and secondary levels are born in the United States, 77 percent and 56 percent respectively. Finally, the overwhelming majority, between 75 and 80 percent, speak Spanish as the primary language.

Beyond enrollments, however, is the devastating reality of segregation and poverty. The Urban Institute reported in 2005 that 70 percent of emergent bilinguals are concentrated in just 10 percent of schools, usually in urban and poor areas. This "super-segregation" meant that in schools with an emergent bilingual population of 25 percent or more (known as "high ELL [English language learners] schools"), 77 percent of students are students of color and more than half are Latino. Moreover, upwards of three-quarters received free and reduced-price lunches, the federal measure of poverty in schools. In fact, 75 percent of emergent bilinguals are poor.

Not only are these super-segregated schools financially poor, but they also have the most poorly trained staff. The Urban Institute report found that only 53 percent of teachers in "high ELL schools" were fully certified, compared to 76 percent in other schools. Another study of the 1.2 million teachers (about 43 percent of all teachers) with emergent bilinguals in their classrooms found that: only 11 percent were certified in bilingual education, with another 18 percent certified in English as a second language; only 15 percent were fluent in another language; and on average, these teachers received four hours of in-service training for working with emergent bilinguals over *the previous five years*. To be clear: the point here is not to lay the deplorable education of emergent bilinguals at teachers' feet—although racist attitudes among some teachers exist and matter—but rather to expose an education system that cares so little about the educational and linguistic needs of emergent bilinguals that it doesn't bother to prepare teachers to work with them.

Language Spoken at Home and English-Speaking Ability Among Foreign-Born Hispanics, by Date of Arrival and Age: 2008

	Younger Than 18				18 and Older			
	Only English spoken at home	Lang, other than only English at home			Only English spoken at home	Lang, other than only English at home		
		English spoken very well	English spoken less than very well	Total		English spoken very well	English spoken less than very well	Total
Date of Arrival								
Before 1990	—	—	—	—	344,590	2,240,803	4,297,960	6,883,353
1990 to 1999	21,261	290,039	86,356	397,656	139,660	1,152,530	3,733,750	5,025,940
2000 and later	33,099	425,425	430,392	888,916	140,333	546,249	3,839,083	4,525,665
Total	54,360	715,464	516,748	1,286,572	624,583	3,939,582	11,870,793	16,434,958
Percent Distribution								
Before 1990	—	—	—	—	5.0	32.6	62.4	100.0
1990 to 1999	5.3	72.9	21.7	100.0	2.8	22.9	74.3	100.0
2000 and later	3.7	47.9	48.4	100.0	3.1	12.1	84.8	100.0
All	4.2	55.6	40.2	100.0	3.8	24.0	72.2	100.0

TAKEN FROM: Pew Hispanic Center Tabulations of 2008 American Community Survey.

Bilingual Education Programs

This crisis is seen still more clearly in the structure and funding of academic programs for emergent bilinguals. A recent American Federation of Teachers report found that fully 60 percent of emergent bilinguals are educated in English-only programs. Of that portion, *12 percent receive no additional support whatsoever* in learning English—in most cases in violation of federal law. Many policymakers evade this issue by citing the difficulty in comparing programs state-by-state. There may be differences in terminology from one area to the other, but the reality remains that far too many emergent bilinguals are subjected to the most notorious model of all: sink-or-swim. And not surprisingly, too many sink. The 2001 reauthorization of the Elementary and Secondary Education Act of 1965, more commonly known as No Child Left Behind (NCLB), mandates that all high stakes testing be done in English. Obviously, if you don't understand academic English you're not going to pass. And far too many emergent bilinguals are allowed to give up and drop out of school altogether. Even a quick glance at funding for language education shows why programs are so lacking. While NCLB increased overall federal support for emergent bilingual education from $200 to $700 million dollars, its testing requirements have resulted in a massive shift toward English-only approaches. In addition to federal money, thirty-three states officially provide additional funding for language programs. However, twenty-four of those states do not require these extra funds to be spent on emergent bilinguals specifically. Finally, ten states spend the generous amount of $0 on emergent bilingual education.

One Arizona court case best captures the criminal neglect of English learners. In 1992, the *Flores v. Arizona* lawsuit was brought against the school district in the border town of Nogales. The plaintiffs accused the district of allotting too little money and too few qualified staff for emergent bilingual programs. That case has endured an epic odyssey through the state and federal courts ever since. A series of rulings has ordered the state legislature to increase state funding for language education. The Republican-controlled State House and Arizona Department of Education (ADE) have resisted at every step. In response to the most recent ruling, ADE and the legislature promised $40 million more in funding—a mere $250 per student—if schools implemented a new model called Structured English Immersion. Under this model, all emergent bilinguals are segregated from the mainstream population for four hours a day—two-thirds of the typical school day—and "submerged" in English-only, grammar-based instruction in reading, writing, and oral skills. The latest court challenge was successful in declaring the funding for this reactionary model insufficient. But ADE appealed to the Supreme Court, which heard the case but returned it last June to the lower courts, leaving the central issues in legal limbo.

Bilingualism and Bilingual Education

This shift back to English-only approaches to educating emergent bilinguals flies in the face of over forty years' worth of applied linguistic research on the benefits of bilingualism and bilingual education. Certainly, some English-only proponents, such as Kevin Clark, attempt to dress up their arguments with "science." However, as renowned applied linguists Stephen Krashen, Kellie Rolstad, and Jeff MacSwan have shown, such arguments are based on turning the research on its head, if not also by telling outright lies. To be sure, there are important debates in applied linguistics about how best to foster multilingualism: at what age, what sort of models and materials, etc. Nevertheless, the balance of research is irrefutable in terms of the benefits of bilingualism and bilingual education.

Not only do bilinguals have access to the various cultures associated with the languages they speak, but also their language skills tend to lead to greater appreciation of human diversity. This is related to the ability for communicative sensitivity. By understanding that there are multiple ways to say similar things, bilinguals have been shown to be more sensitive to the needs of the person(s) interacting with them. Moreover, bilinguals have been shown to be more flexible in their thinking and more adept at thinking about how they use language to get their point across. Additionally, bilinguals have been shown to be more effective at creative and divergent thinking. Finally, the research is unequivocal that literacy in the first language makes learning a second language—and becoming literate in that language—much easier. In fact, once a second language is learned, bilinguals often are able to learn additional languages more easily. Taken together, these findings in the research are often boiled down to claiming that bilinguals are "smarter." This is not really provable, but is tied to the fact that bilinguals tend to outperform monolinguals on standardized testing, whatever the faults of such testing may be.

Models of Bilingual Education

Even if we accept that bilingualism is beneficial, *bilingual education* is much more controversial. In fact, there are many models of bilingual education. The predominant model in the U.S. since the 1960s has been transitional bilingual education. This model is based on the finding just discussed, that children learn a second language more effectively when they are literate in their first language. Therefore, transitional models often target students in the early grades, generally K–3, and use the home language to learn English more effectively. Typically, the home language is used in the early grades 90 percent of the time and English for 10 percent of the time. By grade three, those ratios are reversed, and students then progress to English-only classrooms thereafter. This approach to English language learning has as its goal English language acquisition, not developing the home language. In practice, these models are meant only for language minority students. As such, they are predicated on a deficit model, that is, that non-English proficiency is a problem to remediate through temporary bilingual education.

By contrast, maintenance or developmental models, as their names suggest, are based on maintaining proficiency (and developing literacy) in the home language while developing proficiency and literacy in a second language. Such models are often known as dual language or two-way language classrooms. Not only are the goals of these programs different from transitional models in terms of maintaining and expanding the home language, but these classrooms integrate English monolingual students learning a second language with language minority students learning English, each group learning from the other.

Elite Programs

Of course, there are long-standing elite programs in bilingual education as well. Such programs are often set up in private schools, or as magnet programs within public systems, and target English monolinguals as their main audience. These programs speak to the schizophrenic nature of language education in the United States. "Foreign language" education, i.e. English monolinguals learning additional languages at school whether through bilingual models or not, has existed for over 100 years as a gatekeeping project to get into university. From its first days in an expanding secondary school system at the turn of the twentieth century through today, successful "foreign language" education is often a function of middle- or ruling-class status and considered an elite project for the college-bound. Students who enter school, however, already fluent in a non-English language, are construed as a problem, at times even an outright threat. The balance of the twelve years of schooling functions to rob students of their language and replace it with academic English.

Objections to bilingual education take on several forms and express many myths—sometimes argued by parents of emergent bilinguals themselves. For example, exposing children to too many languages at once will confuse them; learning more than one language means that no language is learned well; children will only learn the minority language, and not English, and thus lead to social isolation or thwart upward mobility, etc. Some of these myths are based on genuine confusion about language learning. More of them are based on political arguments against *the speakers* of non-English languages. . . . It is important to underscore that no recent research comparing English-only versus bilingual models has found English-only approaches to be more effective at teaching English. In fact, most program model comparisons have shown bilingual models to be more effective for *acquisition* of English.

"*The stereotype of the welfare-dependent Latino illegal immigrant appears to have replaced the black inner-city welfare recipient . . . in the imagination of many Americans suspicious of further expansion of the federal social insurance system.*"

Racial Resentment of Latinos Fuels Opposition to Health-Care Reform

Michael Lind

Michael Lind is policy director of the Economic Growth Program at the New America Foundation. In the following viewpoint, he contends that opposition to health care is based in racial resentment. Since the founding of the United States, Lind argues, social welfare programs have had a direct connection to racial politics.

As you read, consider the following questions:

1. In 2008, what percentage of the US gross domestic product (GDP) was spent on social programs, according to Lind?

Michael Lind, "Uninsured Like Me," Salon.com, September 15, 2009. This article first appeared in Salon.com at http://www.salon.com. An online version remains in the *Salon* archives. Reprinted with permission.

2. What percentage of their GDP do Sweden and France spend on social programs, as reported by the author?

3. According to Lind, since the passage of what major piece of legislation has every attempt to expand traditional social insurance in America failed?

Now and then a moment occurs that clarifies the nature of American politics like a flash of lightning over a prairie landscape. Such a moment occurred on Sept. 9 [2009] during President Obama's televised address to a joint session of Congress about healthcare. As the president explained that illegal immigrants would not be eligible for benefits under the plan he supported, Joe Wilson, a conservative Republican member of Congress from South Carolina, shocked the chamber and the television audience by shouting, "You lie!"

Set aside the rich symbolism of the fact that the nation's first black president was rudely challenged by a conservative politician from South Carolina, the most radical of the antebellum Southern slave states, the home of John C. Calhoun, theorist of states' rights and slavery, the place where the first shot of the Civil War was fired at Fort Sumter. In a blazing moment the incident illuminated the continuing entanglement of the politics of race and the welfare state in America.

The Politics of Social Welfare

The American social insurance system is minimal compared not only to the countries of Scandinavia and continental Europe but also to other English-speaking nations like Britain and Canada, both of which have universal healthcare programs. In 2008, the U.S. spent only 19 percent of GDP [gross domestic product] on social programs, compared to nearly 30 percent in both Sweden and France.

From the beginning, attempts to create a universal welfare state in the U.S. have been thwarted by the fears of voters that they will be taxed to subsidize other Americans who are unlike them in race or ethnicity or culture. The original Social Security Act passed only after domestic workers and farmworkers—the majority of black Americans, in the 1930s—were left out of its coverage, at the insistence of white Southern politicians. Aid to Families With Dependent Children, a New Deal antipoverty program that became identified in the public mind with nonwhite "welfare queens," was a target of popular resentment for half a century before it was finally abolished by the Republican Congress and President Bill Clinton in the 1990s.

Racial resentments undoubtedly explain the use of "redistribution" and "socialism" as code words by John McCain, Sarah Palin and Republican working-class mascot "Joe the Plumber" during the 2008 presidential campaign. Similar themes have surfaced during the healthcare debate. Among the many popular fears that conservative opponents of healthcare reform play upon is the anxiety that elderly working Americans will have their Medicare benefits cut, or might even be encouraged to volunteer for euthanasia, to subsidize healthcare for the country's 12 million or so permanently resident illegal immigrants: "Kill Grandma to pay for Pedro."

The Fear of the Other

The Stereotype of the welfare-dependent Latino illegal immigrant appears to have replaced the black inner-city welfare recipient as the "other" in the imagination of many Americans suspicious of further expansion of the federal social insurance system. This explains Rep. Wilson's outburst that President Obama had to be lying when he said that illegal immigrants would not benefit from healthcare reform. Another conservative Republican named Wilson, former California Gov. Pete Wilson, prospered politically from the native white backlash against welfare for illegal immigrants in California in the early 1990s, although the Republican Party subsequently suffered from alienating the state's growing Latino electorate. The Austin Lounge Lizards said it best, in their song "Teenage Immigrant Welfare Mothers on Drugs":

All those teenage immigrant welfare mothers on drugs

(They're on the Dole)

Teenage immigrant welfare mothers on drugs

(They're speaking espanol)

Since the 1964 Civil Rights Act destroyed formal white supremacy in the U.S., every attempt to expand traditional social insurance in America has failed. Meanwhile, there has been a massive expansion in government-sponsored welfare going disproportionately to the white and affluent. What the political scientist Christopher Howard calls the hidden welfare state includes the tax-favored employer-provided health insurance that most working-age Americans depend on, as well as the home mortgage interest deduction and the childcare and child tax credits. Affluent and educated workers are more likely to work for employers who provide private health benefits than are low-skilled workers and employees of small businesses. Personal tax benefits like the home mortgage interest deduction are available only to the top half of households who pay federal income taxes, and are unavailable to lower-income workers who pay payroll taxes but no income taxes. In many cases, the benefits of this tax-credit welfare state increase with income.

There is even a nonrefundable "childcare tax credit" available only to the relatively affluent families who pay income taxes in addition to payroll taxes. There's no publicly provided or subsidized daycare to help out the nanny who takes care of the rich brat, but the taxpayers subsidize the rich brat's parents when they employ the nanny.

Ethnic Nepotism?

Is it a coincidence that following the Civil Rights Act white Americans stopped expanding the traditional welfare state and instead started building a private, income-based welfare state for themselves? Could it be pure coincidence that the most generous welfare states in the world have been those of ethnically homogeneous Nordic countries where, until recent immigration, nearly everyone was related to everyone else? Is the classic welfare state really a form of ethnic nepotism most likely to be adopted by a homogeneous, indeed tribal, nation-state?

Recent scholarship supports the hypothesis that ethnic diversity tends to be inversely correlated with generous, universal social insurance. In a 2001 paper titled "Why Doesn't the US Have a European-Style Welfare State?" Alberto Alesina, Edward Glaeser and Bruce Sacerdote wrote that "race is critically important to understanding the US-Europe differences" and that "hostility to welfare comes in part from the fact that welfare spending in the US goes disproportionately to minorities."

Social Security and Medicare, the two major examples of universal social insurance in the U.S., were enacted during a half-century between World War I and the 1970s when the foreign-born percentage of the U.S. population was at an all-time low and ethnic differences were fading rapidly in a white majority that made up a secure nine-tenths of the population. Arguably a sense of post-ethnic, pan-white nationalism, combined with a small nonwhite majority consisting almost entirely of African-Americans, is one of the reasons, if not the major reason, that the U.S. came closer to European social democracy between 1932 and 1968 than in the periods of greater immigration and cultural heterogeneity that came before and afterward.

The Challenge for Democrats

The tension between diversity and solidarity is a problem for both wings of the Democratic Party in the United States. In an increasingly diverse society with population growth driven by immigration, it will be even harder for the social democrats on the left wing of the Democratic Party to persuade the dwindling number of native white voters of the merits of universal policies that could benefit both them and the newcomers.

> "Welcome to post-racial America, where those who oppose [health-care reform] must defend themselves against the scurrilous charges of a man who seems much better suited to reviewing Cats."

Calling Opposition to Health Care Racist Is Shameful

Pat Sajak

Pat Sajak is a political commentator and a television game-show host. In the following viewpoint, he counters a recent claim by New York Times *columnist Frank Rich that opposition to President Barack Obama's health-care plan is based in racial resentment against minorities. Sajak asserts that the topic of health care should be debated on its merits instead of distorted by charges of racism and sexism from the left.*

As you read, consider the following questions:

1. What position did Frank Rich occupy for many years at the *New York Times*, according to Sajak?

2. Rich, as quoted by the author, compares the opposition to health-care reform to the reaction to what other piece of federal legislation?

Pat Sajak, "Opposed to Obamacare? Then You Must Be a Racist," *Human Events*, March 29, 2010. Reproduced by permission.

3. According to Sajak, how many Americans oppose Obama's health-care reform?

Frank Rich spent many years as the theater critic for the *New York Times*, where, at worst, his venom could cause a Broadway production or two to close down.

Now, however, Mr. Rich opines on political and social issues for the *Times*, and, while the results are usually mildly amusing (even if unintentionally so), his reach has grown a bit, so the damage he causes can travel beyond the footlights. I'm not sure why anyone turns to Rich for political analysis—heck, you might as well read the rantings of a TV game show host—but the Gray Lady [a nickname for the *New York Times*] continues to pay him for his weekly column, and, at the rate she's bleeding money, that's no small sacrifice.

Anyway, Mr. Rich has apparently been able to get to the bottom of the vocal opposition to the "healthcare reform" bill that was recently gently shepherded through Congress.

It turns out, according to his well-crafted analysis, that it's not the bill that's got people in an uproar; rather, what we're facing is the death rattle of a dwindling cadre of white, racist, sexist, homophobic males terrified by the ascent of people of color, women and gays.

As the ever-tolerant Rich reasons: "The conjunction of a black President and a female speaker of the House—topped off by a wise Latina on the Supreme Court and a powerful gay congressional committee chairman—would sow fears of disenfranchisement among a dwindling and threatened minority in the country no matter what policies were in play."

Racism to Blame?

So that's it. It's just a bunch of scared, white males who would yelp about anything this gang came up with. As Rich makes clear, this is merely a replay of the opposition to the Voting Rights Act of 1964. You get it? If you express opposition to the bill, you're a racist, sexist homophobe.

Persons Without Health Insurance, by Age, Race, and Ethnicity: 2008

	Persons Without Health Insurance			
	Younger than 18	18 to 64	65 and older	Total
Hispanic	2,985,446	11,687,954	178,122	14,851,522
Native born	2,252,578	3,641,893	23,963	5,918,434
Foreign born	732,868	8,046,061	154,159	8,933,088
White alone, not Hispanic	2,739,263	18,394,663	213,855	21,347,781
Black alone, not Hispanic	1,006,876	5,909,127	77,860	6,993,863
Asian alone, not Hispanic	269,464	1,591,211	78,406	1,939,081
Other, not Hispanic	353,316	1,223,825	19,249	1,596,390
Total	7,354,365	38,806,780	567,492	46,728,637

	Uninsured Rate (%)			
	Younger than 18	18 to 64	65 and older	Total
Hispanic	18.7	41.5	6.8	31.7
Native born	15.4	27.7	2.0	20.4
Foreign born	52.3	53.6	10.9	50.1
White alone, not Hispanic	6.6	14.6	0.7	10.7
Black alone, not Hispanic	9.8	25.3	2.4	19.0
Asian alone, not Hispanic	9.3	17.6	6.2	14.7
Other, not Hispanic	10.6	27.4	4.1	19.3
All	10.0	20.3	1.5	15.4

TAKEN FROM: Pew Hispanic Center Tabulations of 2008 American Community Survey.

Mr. Rich is shocked by the level of anger in the land, and he fears for the safety of our elected officials, much as I'm sure he did during the George W. Bush administration. He calls on Republican leaders to distance themselves from the more radical voices among them, echoing the demands I'm sure he made of the Democrats during the last campaign.

Welcome to post-racial America, where those who oppose a piece of legislation must defend themselves against the scurrilous charges of a man who seems much better suited to reviewing *Cats*. (He liked it, by the way.) This was a particularly shameful column, and the millions of Americans who oppose this legislation are owed an apology. Are they right? Are they wrong? Let's discuss it. Let's debate it. Let's yell and scream if we want to. But would it be too much to ask that we approach the matter based on its merits and leave the psychobabble to Dr. Phil?

| "As the wealth of Hispanic residents continues to grow, both local and national companies are likely to pay more and more attention to this important market segment."

Companies Are Increasingly Targeting the Burgeoning Latino Market

Sarah Dougherty

Sarah Dougherty is an economic analyst for the Federal Reserve Bank of Atlanta. In the following viewpoint, she maintains that US companies have discovered the potential of the growing Hispanic consumer market. Dougherty reports that many companies, especially in the communications industry, are conducting research in order to effectively target their goods and services to this increasingly prosperous demographic.

As you read, consider the following questions:

1. As of 2003, how many Hispanics lived in the Southeast, according to Dougherty?

2. As reported by the author, what was the buying power of Hispanics in the Southeast in 2003?

Sarah Dougherty, "Riding the Rising Wave of Hispanic Buying Power," *EconSouth*, vol. 7, 2005. Reproduced by permission.

3. According to the Inter-American Development Bank as cited by Dougherty, how much money have Hispanics sent back to their home countries in Latin America?

As the Southeast population continues to grow, one segment in particular is outpacing all other groups: the Hispanic population. According to the U.S. Census the population of the United States as a whole was 283 million in 2003, an increase of 14 percent from 1990. Over the same time period the Hispanic population rose 75 percent and now stands at around 39 million. In the Southeast, the change has been even more dramatic. The Southeastern population was about 42 million in 2003, up 20 percent from 1990, whereas the Hispanic segment swelled 116 percent to 4 million in 2003. Some believe even this growth in the Hispanic population may be understated because many illegal Hispanic immigrants are not included in the official Census data.

The rapid Hispanic population growth has led to an increase in economic importance. For instance, according to Enrique J. Moras, vice president of acquisition banking for Wachovia Corp., Hispanic households with more than $100,000 in annual earnings are growing at more than twice the pace of the general population. This increasing Hispanic buying power is a point not lost on retailers and other businesses. But if marketers want to capture a share of this burgeoning market segment, they need to discover how the Hispanic community differs from other markets and use this information to focus their strategies. Some companies, especially in the communications industry, have been quite active in targeting the Hispanic market.

Pocketbook Power

Buying power—personal disposable income, or after-tax income available for purchasing goods and services—is a measure of the relative economic importance of a market segment. Dr. Raul Perez, president of Utilis Research, a marketing research firm in New York, estimates that the buying power of Hispanics in the Southeast grew threefold from 1990 to 2003, from $24 billion to $79 billion, while the buying power of the general population increased twofold, from $528 billion to $1.045 trillion. "The percent of total buying power in the Southeast attributed to Hispanics grew from just over 4 percent to over 7 percent in the same period," he said.

Florida has long been among the top states in the nation with significant Hispanic markets. Officially, the Hispanic population in Florida stood at around 3.1 million in 2003, an increase of some 1.5 million since 1990. Over the same period, the buying power of the state's Hispanic residents grew by an estimated $40 billion. Georgia also has a considerable Hispanic population, totaling around 531,000 in 2003, almost a fivefold increase from the estimated 109,000 Hispanics in the state in 1990. What's more, the buying power of Georgia Hispanics has grown an estimated $9 billion since 1990, when it was only $1 billion, according to the Selig Center of the University of Georgia. In Alabama, Louisiana, and Mississippi, the Hispanic population is also growing rapidly but nonetheless remains relatively small.

Analysts project that Hispanic buying power will reach 9 percent of the nation's total buying power by the end of this decade [2009]. A number of research studies suggest that Hispanic buying power should increase more than fivefold in the Southeast toward the end of the decade. And indications are that the Hispanic boom will not slow down after that time. If this boom takes shape as expected, it will represent a huge opportunity for new and existing businesses to increase sales and customers. . . .

A Piece of the Pie

Businesses are beginning to sit up and take notice. While plenty of Hispanic-focused companies have been marketing and selling directly to Latino consumers for years, a number of larger, traditionally non-Hispanic-focused companies are now actively working to carve out a piece of the Hispanic market.

The communications industry is a prime example. On Feb. 2 [2005], WEBG-FM in Orlando became that city's first completely Spanish-language station with its new moniker, Rumba 100.3. Linda Byrd, a regional vice president for central and north Florida at Clear Channel Communications, a large media company and parent of WEBG, commented that "Orlando is one of the fastest-growing Hispanic markets in the nation and one of the largest [radio markets], with 20 percent of listeners being Hispanic." Clear Channel is switching 25 of its radio stations nationwide to Spanish-language formats by the end of 2005, bringing its Spanish-language initiative to a total of 39 radio stations in the United States.

Telecommunications companies that currently serve Latinos, such as Univision Communications Inc. and the Spanish Broadcasting System, are also seeing their markets grow. Larger companies are now seeing enough critical mass in the Hispanic market to make it worth their while to increase their presence in that market segment. Advertising industry analysts anticipate that revenue for Spanish-speaking markets will grow rapidly as more companies focus their messages to reach Hispanic audiences.

Hispanic Television

Hispanic television has already experienced a dramatic expansion: Of the 75 Hispanic pay television stations, 33 were launched in the past two years [2003–2005]. Several have come from big-name media companies, such as CNN, Fox, and MTV, and others are broadcast directly from Latin American countries. Local channels are also starting up to serve Hispanic communities. WUVG Univision 24, which began broadcasting in the Atlanta area in 2002, is Georgia's only Spanish-language local broadcast television station.

Spanish-Language Newspapers

Spanish-language newspapers are vying for space on retailers' shelves. Several larger markets such as Los Angeles, Dallas, Miami, and New York have their own Spanish-language dailies produced by larger, established newspaper publishers. In other markets, small, family-owned newspapers have generally dominated. Luis Espinoza, of Jackson, Miss., started *La Noticia* last year [2004], a weekly, 12-page tabloid distributed to community centers and Hispanic restaurants and grocery stores. "My goal is eventually to publish more news about and for Latinos in the area," he said.

But media companies are not the only ones noticing the growth potential of the Hispanic market. The market once left to smaller companies who specialize in Hispanic-focused products now attracts major players. Publix Super Markets, based in Lakeland, Fla., is adding Hispanic products to its private line in the next few months. With all of its 849 stores in the Southeast, Publix believes it has a ripe audience to compete against established Hispanic food producers, such as Badia and Goya Foods.

Tapping Unbanked Wealth

The financial sector also appears to be primed for growth among the Hispanic population. According to the Pew Hispanic Center, 24 percent of Hispanics in this country are unbanked. Of Latinos in the United States who send remittances, notes the Pew Center, 55 percent have no credit cards and 43 percent have no bank accounts. According to Manuel Orozco of Inter-American Dialogue, there is broad mistrust of banks by Latinos. Some studies also suggest that the unbanked are also illegal immigrants afraid of the banking system.

Households, by Income, Race, and Ethnicity: 2008

	1st quintile (up to $21,793)	2nd quintile ($21,794–$40,755)	3rd quintile ($40,756–$65,176)	4th quintile ($65,177–$101,839)	5th quintile ($101,840+)	Total
Hispanic	3,105,546	3,178,314	2,673,879	2,173,214	1,478,559	12,609,512
Native born	1,414,764	1,286,236	1,212,010	1,133,704	858,407	5,905,121
Foreign born	1,690,782	1,892,078	1,461,869	1,039,510	620,152	6,704,391
White alone, not Hispanic	13,971,555	15,257,835	16,305,273	17,211,942	18,202,767	80,949,372
Black alone, not Hispanic	4,272,325	3,153,815	2,470,774	1,976,538	1,251,876	13,125,328
Asian alone, not Hispanic	662,354	600,785	703,575	906,832	1,331,021	4,204,567
Other, not Hispanic	563,645	469,391	427,481	413,855	336,974	2,211,346
Total	22,575,425	22,660,140	22,580,982	22,682,381	22,601,197	113,100,125
Percent Distribution						
Hispanic	24.6	25.2	21.2	17.2	11.7	100.0
Native born	24.0	21.8	20.5	19.2	14.5	100.0
Foreign born	25.2	28.2	21.8	15.5	9.2	100.0
White alone, not Hispanic	17.3	18.8	20.1	21.3	22.5	100.0
Black alone, not Hispanic	32.6	24.0	18.8	15.1	9.5	100.0
Asian alone, not Hispanic	15.8	14.3	16.7	21.6	31.7	100.0
Other, not Hispanic	25.5	21.2	19.3	18.7	15.2	100.0
All	20.0	20.0	20.0	20.1	20.0	100.0

TAKEN FROM: Pew Hispanic Center Tabulations of 2008 American Community Survey.

The big financial institutions throughout the Southeast are reaching out to the Latino market with new services or existing services repackaged to address the unique needs of this market. According to Moras, Wachovia Bank's footprint covers fully 30 percent of the overall Hispanic population in key markets like Miami. He says that Hispanics represent an underserved segment, with nearly 40 percent of this market having no traditional banking relationship. To reach this large and growing market segment, Wachovia has identified four areas on which to concentrate its market development efforts: human resources to foster employees who relate to the segment, marketing, focused product development, and community involvement, Moras notes.

Smaller banks are also beginning to target the Hispanic market in the Southeast. Independent banks like Atlanta-based United Americas Bank are catering to the Latino market. "One of our primary goals is to help first-time homebuyers in the Hispanic market to acquire their homes. Our experience has been very good to date. We've seen people in our target market show tremendous pride in the idea of home ownership, and, consequently, our delinquency rates have been very, very low," said Jorge Forment, president of United Americas.

Know Thy Market

For companies considering entering the Hispanic market or expanding their market focus, differences in spending patterns are key. In many cases Hispanics are more likely to buy goods and services from other Hispanics in their community. "Relationships are extremely important in the Hispanic culture. If you treat Hispanic customers with both respect and cultural understanding, they will remain loyal to your business and tell their friends and family that you have gone the extra mile to make them feel welcomed," said Maritza Pichon, executive director of the Latin American Association of Atlanta. These Hispanic businesses are also more likely to hire Latino employees, keeping Hispanic dollars within the community. This practice allows employees to gain experience and companies to gain capital and profits.

It is important for businesses striving to enter the Hispanic market to understand some of its demographic differences. For instance, the age profile of the Hispanic community is dramatically younger than that of the general population. Forty-two percent of all U.S. residents are under the age of 30, according to the 2000 Census. In the Hispanic population, 58 percent are under age 30.

Expanding in the Hispanic Market

The age and spending profiles of the growing Hispanic population provide useful indicators of where and how companies can expand in this market. For example, much data suggest that young Hispanic males are sending a significant portion of their wages back to their home countries in Latin America— $30 billion in 2003, according to the Inter-American Development Bank. Assuming these data are accurate, banks might find growth potential in focusing on banking remittances and transfer payments to not only cities but also villages in rural Latin America. Several U.S. banks, including Wells Fargo and Citibank, have acquired or partnered with Latin banks and vice versa in hopes of capturing more of this remittance market from traditionally higher-fee providers. By offering lower transfer costs, banks offering remittance services are gaining ground.

Trying to profit from the demographic differences of the Hispanic population is not limited to remittance senders. For example, Census figures show that 31 percent of Hispanic households had five or more people and that 35 percent of the total Latino population is under the age of 18. This youthful market provides opportunities for companies whose products and services are aimed at children. An A.C. Nielsen study shows that market penetration for items typically bought by and for children and teens averaged 38 percent higher for Hispanic households than for non-Hispanic white households.

As the wealth of Hispanic residents continues to grow both local and national companies are likely to pay more and more attention to this important market segment. Companies can learn to tailor their products to take advantage of the different demographic and cultural considerations of the rapidly growing Latino market. Media companies are already positioning themselves to benefit from the advertising dollars that will flow as the result of expanding Hispanic buying power. Waiting until Hispanics have become an even larger, established market may mean missed opportunities.

Periodical and Internet Sources Bibliography

The following articles have been selected to supplement the diverse views presented in this chapter.

Carrie Budoff Brown	"Hispanic Democrats Want Health Care Fix," *Politico*, July 19, 2010.
Andrew Edgecliffe-Johnson	"Marketing: Not Yet Wrapped Up," *Financial Times*, September 7, 2010.
Lance Izumi	"Remembering Prop. 227 and the 'End' of Bilingual Education," *FlashReport*, June 18, 2008.
Ezra Klein	"How Race Affects Attitudes Towards Obama, Health Care," *Washington Post*, January 11, 2010.
Bruno Korschek	"Is Opposition to President Obama's Health Care More About Race?" Helium.com, September 18, 2010. www.helium.com.
Louis Llovio	"Hispanics Key to Rebound, U.S. Treasurer Says," *Richmond (VA) Times-Dispatch*, September 15, 2010.
Natalia Lopera	"Hispanic Market Demystified," *Arizona Daily Star*, September 17, 2010.
Ruben Navarrette Jr.	"'English-Only Debate' Rule Lost in Translation," CNN.com, September 10, 2007. http://articles.cnn.com.
Alexandra Sabater	"Bilingual Education Can Benefit All Students," *Dallas Morning News*, September 10, 2010.
Harris R. Sherline	"The Case for English Only," GOPUSA.com, June 23, 2008. www.gopusa.com.

For Further Discussion

Chapter 1

1. How do you characterize the Hispanic contribution to life in the United States? Reread the viewpoints by Carolee Walker and Steve Sailer to inform your opinion.

2. In his viewpoint, Alberto Gonzales argues that Latino values are conservative family values. Heather Mac Donald disagrees, contending that such characterizations are superficial and do not take into account statistics about Hispanic families and education. How do you view Latino values after reading both viewpoints? Cite from the viewpoints in your answer.

Chapter 2

1. Do you believe Arizona's immigration law is racist? In his viewpoint, Alvaro Huerta argues that it is, whereas Bruce Maiman maintains it is not. Reread both perspectives and formulate a position of your own.

2. Barbara Simpson maintains that undocumented Latino immigrants raise the US crime rates. In his viewpoint, Ron Unz counters Simpson's assertion and argues that the crime rates for Latinos are about the same as for whites. Is Simpson's argument viable? Why or why not? Use the information provided by the viewpoints to support your opinion.

3. There is a growing movement in the United States to end birthright citizenship. After reading the viewpoints by George Will and Eric Foner that present arguments on both sides of the issue, what is your position on birthright citizenship?

Chapter 3

1. Jennifer Parker maintains that Democrats are attracting Latino voters in order to win elections. Star Parker argues that Republicans must attract Latino voters, too. Who needs Latino voters more in your opinion? Why?

2. Do you think Latino voters will make a significant difference in the next presidential election? Why or why not? Reread the viewpoints of Alex Koppelman and Steve Sailer before you give your opinion, citing from their arguments.

Chapter 4

1. Heather Mac Donald argues that bilingual education works against the Hispanic community because it functions to hinder assimilation. Jeff Bale, however, maintains that it is still the best approach to education for those still learning English. Which viewpoint best represents your opinion on the subject and why?

2. Health-care reform was one of the major political issues of 2009 and 2010. what role did racial resentment play in the health-care debate in your opinion? Reread the viewpoints by Pat Sajak and Michael Lind to inform your answer.

Organizations to Contact

The editors have compiled the following list of organizations concerned with the issues debated in this book. The descriptions are derived from materials provided by the organizations. All have publications or information available for interested readers. The list was compiled on the date of publication of the present volume; the information provided here may change. Be aware that many organizations take several weeks or longer to respond to inquiries, so allow as much time as possible.

Congressional Hispanic Caucus Institute (CHCI)
911 Second Street NE, Washington, DC   20002
(202) 543-1771 • fax: (202) 546-2143
website: www.chci.org

The Congressional Hispanic Caucus Institute is a nonprofit, nonpartisan leadership development organization for the Hispanic community. It works to promote educational opportunities, offer leadership training programs, and give leadership experience to the next generation of Hispanic civic and political leaders. One of its most important programs is the CHCI scholarship programs for qualified Hispanic students. It also sponsors a Congressional Hispanic internship program. The CHCI website provides updated information on recent events, including video and pictures.

Federation for American Immigration Reform (FAIR)
25 Massachusetts Ave. NW, Suite 330, Washington, DC   20001
(202) 328-7004 • fax: (202) 387-3447
website: www.fairus.org

FAIR is a national, nonprofit membership organization that lobbies for improved border security and tougher immigration laws. One of the main ways it accomplishes this is through research and studies used by academics, politicians, lobbyists, and the media to influence the national conversation on immigration. Recent publications include *Immigration and National Security: 2010 Update, Immigration and Population Growth in the United States,* and *The Fiscal Burden of Illegal Immigration on U.S. Taxpayers.* It also offers fact sheets and statistics on immigration and immigrants.

Labor Council for Latin American Advancement (LCLAA)
815 Sixteenth Street NW, 4th Floor, Washington, DC   20006
(202) 508-6919 • fax: (202) 508-6922
e-mail: headquarters@lclaa.org
website: www.lclaa.org

The Labor Council for Latin American Advancement (LCLAA) is a national organization devoted to the advancement of Latino union members. LCLAA works toward economic and social justice for workers and promotes diversity and fairness in the workplace. Building coalitions between Latino union members and the trade unions, the LCLAA holds voter registration campaigns and organizes Latino workers to take advantage of economic and social opportunities. The LCLAA publishes *LCLAA Magazine,* which provides an in-depth look at issues relevant to Latino workers. The LCLAA website hosts LCLAA radio, a list of upcoming events, and a picture gallery of past events.

League of United Latin American Citizens (LULAC)
2000 L Street NW, Suite 610, Washington, DC   20036
(202) 833-6130 • fax: (202) 833-6135
website: www.lulac.org

The League of United Latin American Citizens (LULAC) is the nation's oldest Hispanic organization. It advocates for better economic and educational opportunities, better health care, civil rights, and a greater political influence for Hispanics on the national scene. The league's members "provide more than a million dollars in scholarships to Hispanic students each year, conduct citizenship and voter registration drives, develop low-income housing units, conduct youth leadership training programs, and seek to empower the Hispanic community at the local, state, and national levels." LULAC conducts a range of research on a variety of key issues, which are described on the organization's website. It also publishes the *LULAC Civil Rights Manual*, an education e-newsletter, and a blog that explores current events and matters of interest.

Mexican American Legal Defense & Educational Fund (MALDEF)

634 S. Spring Street, Los Angeles, CA   90014
(213) 629-2512
website: www.maldef.org

MALDEF was established in 1968 to be the premier Latino legal civil rights organization. According to the MALDEF website, the group "promotes social change through advocacy, communications, community education, and litigation in the areas of education, employment, immigrant rights, and political access." It focuses on issues of immigration, education, employment, and voting rights. MALDEF offers a range of publications on these issues, including *Listening to Latinas: Barriers to High School Graduation* and *Language Rights*.

MANA: A National Latina Organization

1146 Nineteenth Street NW, Suite 700
Washington, DC   20036
(202) 833-0060 • fax: (202) 496-0588
e-mail: hermana2@aol.com
website: www.hermana.org

Founded in 1974, MANA is a nonprofit advocacy organization dedicated to empowering Latinas through leadership development and community service. The organization designs programs that emphasize building leadership skills. Members become part of a nationwide community network and can take part in educational seminars and conferences. They can also apply for scholarships and grants. MANA publishes a monthly newsletter, and provides access to news releases and event information on its website.

National Alliance for Hispanic Health
1501 Sixteenth Street NW, Washington, DC 20036
(202) 387-5000 • fax: (202) 797-4353
e-mail: alliance@hispanichealth.org
website: www.hispanichealth.org

Established in 1973, the National Alliance for Hispanic Health is a nonprofit organization of health and human services providers that works to improve the health of the US Latino community. The alliance reaches more than 15 million people in the United States. Some of the major programs it has developed are focused in the following areas: arthritis, diabetes, cancer, heart health, and women's health. It also sponsors help lines, which provide information on prenatal care and Hispanic family care. More information on health issues can be found on its website, including publications such as *The Latina Guide to Health* and *Genes, Culture, and Medicine: Bridging Gaps in Treatment for Hispanic Americans.*

National Association of Latino Arts and Culture (NALAC)
1208 Buena Vista Street, San Antonio, TX 78207
(210) 432-3982 • fax: (210) 432-3934
e-mail: info@nalac.org
website: www.nalac.org

The National Association of Latino Arts and Culture is a nonprofit organization established to promote the Latino arts community. One way it accomplishes this is through grant programs, like the NALAC Fund for the Arts. Another way it works to help the Latino art community is through the NALAC Leadership Institute, which strives to empower and train Latino artists and art administrators for leadership positions in the community. NALAC also sponsors regional workshops in cities throughout the country and publishes the online *e-Boletín.*

National Coalition of Latino Clergy and Christian Leaders (CONLAMIC)
PO Box 10345, Washington, DC 20020

(202) 615-7444
e-mail: info@conlamic.org
website: www.conlamic.org

Established in 1998, the National Coalition of Latino Clergy and Christian Leaders (CONLAMIC) was formed to "empower Hispanic clergy to increase civic participation and advance the voice and issues of the Latino Church." It represents twenty thousand churches in thirty-four states. CONLAMIC is also a leading voice on issues pertinent to the Latino community, such as immigration reform and economic and social justice. The CONLAMIC website features statements on these issues, and includes archives of earlier statements. You can also listen to podcasts of CONLAMIC Informa Radio.

National Council of La Raza (NCLR)

1126 Sixteenth Street NW, Washington, DC   20036
(202) 785-1670 • fax: (202) 776-1792
e-mail: comments@nclr.org
website: www.nclr.org

The National Council of La Raza is a nonprofit organization that advocates for better employment and economic opportunities for the Latino community. It also works to reduce poverty and eliminate housing and employment discrimination. NCLR is active in lobbying for immigration reform, developing and implementing health education programs, and building valuable job skills and educational opportunities for Hispanic youth. Research is also a key component of NCLR's mission, and on its website are research studies, fact sheets, in-depth issue analysis, and expert testimony. The website also features a blog, which offers the latest news on NCLR events and initiatives.

United States Hispanic Chamber of Commerce (USHCC)

1424 K Street NW, Suite 401, Washington, DC   20005
(800) USHCC86 • fax: (202) 842-1212
website: www.ushcc.com

The USHCC is the leading Hispanic business organization promoting the economic growth and development of Hispanic entrepreneurs. It serves the Hispanic community by creating business relationships and fostering business partnerships between corporate organizations and Hispanic businesses. Serving the needs of more than 3 million Hispanic-owned businesses in the United States, the USHCC lobbies for legislation and programs that benefit the Hispanic business community and also provides technical assistance to Hispanic business associations and entrepreneurs. It also publishes *Enterprise,* a quarterly magazine featuring news, information, and resources for Hispanic businesspeople; and *Chamber News,* a weekly e-newsletter that provides relevant news on upcoming events, current initiatives, and new programs.

Bibliography of Books

David T. Abalos   *Latinos in the United States.* 2nd ed. South Bend, IN: University of Notre Dame Press, 2007.

Jerome R. Adams   *Greasers and Gringos: The Historical Roots of Anglo-Hispanic Prejudice.* Jefferson, NC: McFarland, 2006.

Herman Badillo   *One Nation, One Standard: An Ex-liberal on How Hispanics Can Succeed Just Like Other Immigrant Groups.* New York: Sentinel, 2006.

Lisa García Bedolla   *Latino Politics.* Cambridge: Polity, 2009.

Cristina Beltrán   *The Trouble with Unity: Latino Politics and the Creation of Identity.* New York: Oxford University Press, 2010.

Laird W. Bergad and Herbert S. Klein   *Hispanics in the United States: A Demographic, Social, and Economic History, 1980–2005.* New York: Cambridge University Press, 2010.

Juana Bordes   *Salsa, Soul, and Spirit: Leadership for a Multicultural Age.* San Francisco: Berrett-Koehler, 2007.

Ernesto Caravantes   *Clipping Their Own Wings: The Incompatibility Between Latino Culture and American Education.* Lanham, MD: Hamilton Books, 2006.

Henry G.
Cisneros, ed.

Latinos and the Nation's Future.
Houston: Arte Publico Press, 2009.

Kathleen M. Coll

*Remaking Citizenship: Latina
Immigrants and New American
Politics.* Stanford, CA: Stanford
University Press, 2010.

Sandra Donovan

The Hispanic American Experience.
Minneapolis: Twenty-First Century
Books, 2011.

Patricia Gándara
and Frances
Contreras

*The Latino Education Crisis: The
Consequences of Failed Social Policies.*
Cambridge, MA: Harvard University
Press, 2009.

F. Chris Garcia
and Gabriel R.
Sanchez

*Hispanics and the U.S. Political
System: Moving into the Mainstream.*
Upper Saddle River, NJ:
Prentice-Hall, 2008.

Jorge J.E. Gracia

Latinos in America. Malden, MA:
Blackwell, 2008.

John Iceland

*Where We Live Now: Immigration and
Race in the United States.* Berkeley
and Los Angeles: University of
California Press, 2009.

Bob Menendez

*Growing American Roots: Why Our
Nation Will Thrive as Our Largest
Minority Flourishes.* New York: New
American Library, 2009.

José Luis Morín

*Latino/a Rights and Justice in the
United States.* 2nd ed. Durham, NC:
Carolina Academic Press, 2009.

Suzanne Oboler   *Latinos and Citizenship: The Dilemma of Belonging.* New York: Palgrave Macmillan, 2008.

Eileen O'Brien   *The Racial Middle: Latinos and Asian Americans Living Beyond the Racial Divide.* New York: New York University Press, 2008.

Jorge Ramos   *The Latino Wave: How Hispanics Are Transforming Politics in America.* New York: Rayo, 2005.

Geraldo Rivera   *The Great Progression: How Hispanics Will Lead America to a New Era of Prosperity.* New York: New American Library, 2009.

Samuel Roll and Marc Irwin   *The Invisible Border: Latinos in America.* Boston: Intercultural Press, 2008.

Miriam Jiménez Román and Juan Flores, eds.   *The Afro-Latin@ Reader: History and Culture in the United States.* Durham, NC: Duke University Press, 2010.

Paul R. Smokowski and Martica Bacallo   *Becoming Bicultural: Risk, Resilience, and Latino Youth.* New York: New York University Press, 2010.

Angharad N. Valdivia   *Latino/as and the Media.* Malden, MA: Polity, 2010.

Ana Celia Zentella, ed.   *Building on Strength: Language and Literacy in Latino Families and Communities.* New York: Teachers College Press, 2005.

Index

mL
6
/11